Wild about Mushrooms

A Few Words of Caution

WILD ABOUT MUSHROOMS is a cookbook for mushroom lovers seeking a greater awareness of the many cultivated and wild mushrooms that are becoming increasingly available in supermarkets and specialty shops. Throughout our cookbook, we refer to the dangers of eating certain mushrooms and the possible confusions between safe and poisonous mushrooms. We have not attempted to describe or illustrate mushrooms for the purpose of *identification.*

We recommend that you rely on your proven produce market when purchasing mushrooms, and suggest that you join a mycological society and learn from the experts. Remember, there is no substitute for common sense and knowledge. It is always wise to exercise caution when purchasing mushrooms—even from large supermarkets—and when receiving mushrooms as gifts from friends.

Bon Appetit!

Wild about Mushrooms

A Cookbook
for Feasters
and Foragers

Louise Freedman
with William Freedman
and The Mycological Society
of San Francisco

Illustrations by Teeda LoCodo
Scientific advisors: Harry Thiers, Ph.D., Fred Stevens, Ph.D.

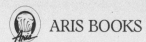 ARIS BOOKS

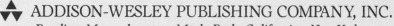 ADDISON-WESLEY PUBLISHING COMPANY, INC.
Reading, Massachusetts   Menlo Park, California   New York
Don Mills, Ontario   Wokingham, England   Amsterdam   Bonn
Sydney   Singapore   Tokyo   Madrid   San Juan.

Dedicated to Charles Sharp, 1910–1984, the editor of *Kitchen Magic with Mushrooms.* The Mycological Society of San Francisco is grateful for his enhancement of our awareness and appreciation of the finer culinary aspects of mushrooms.

Library of Congress Cataloging-in-Publication Data

Freedman, Louise.
  Wild about mushrooms.

  "Aris books."
  Bibliography: p.
  Includes index.
  1. Cookery (Mushrooms) 2. Mushrooms, Edible.   I. Freedman, William, 1919– II. Mycological Society of San Francisco. (Calif.)   III. Title.
TX804.F72   1988   641.6′58   88-8058
ISBN 0-201-19188-1 (pbk.)   Rev.

(Previously published by Harris Publishing Co., ISBN 0-943186-30-7)

Aris Books Editorial Office
and Test Kitchen
1621 Fifth Street
Berkeley, CA 94710
(415) 527-5171

Edited by Carolyn Miller
Designed by Seventeenth Street Studios
Typeset in Leamington by Another Point

Manufactured in the United States of America

First Addison-Wesley Printing, January 1989

ABCDEFGHIJ-DO-89

Contents

Part Four: A Cook's Mushroom Miscellany

Preface

THERE IS evidence that hunter-gatherer humans living in temperate climates have been collecting mushrooms for food for thousands of years.Today, foraging for fungi continues to be an enjoyable family activity in many European and Asiatic countries. Grandparents equipped with basket, knife, cane, and traditional wisdom still instruct their eager children and grandchildren in the techniques and lore of separating edible from non-edible mushrooms. When people migrated to the new world, they brought the excitement and pleasure of this pursuit to America.

The first American mushroom society was formed in Boston in 1895. There now are sixty-seven mycological societies in the United States and Canada. Membership and enthusiasm in these groups continue to grow. In 1950, the Mycological Society of San Francisco was organized to provide an opportunity for interested individuals in the Bay Area to study the fascinating subject of mushrooms and to safely enhance the pleasure of eating them. Each year the tempo of our members' lives quickens as the first autumn rains fall and the objects of our devotion lift their multicolored heads from the ground. The *Mycena News,* MSSF's monthly publication, announces the coming events for the season. Monthly speakers and gourmet dinners are planned. Cultivation and identification classes begin. Field forays and trips local and remote are announced. Dr. Harry Thiers, the mycologist at San Francisco State University, and informed society members identify mushrooms for the public and for medical clinics as a community service. Other members present slide shows for natural science and medical organizations in the area.

But nothing we do approaches the excitement of preparing and participating two or three times each winter in mushroom exhibitions called "fungus fairs." Members gather fungi, then discuss them with people who come to examine the beautifully arranged and labeled mushroom exhibits.

Joining a mushroom society is one of the safest ways to begin the quest for wild mushrooms. A list of mushroom clubs is supplied in Part IV of this book.

Acknowledgments

THIS COOKBOOK took five years to research, organize, and write. Many people have generously helped me, often when I needed it most. Mycological Society members made suggestions and contributed recipes as we worked on the book. You will see their names below their favorite recipes. I would like to thank them all, and I hope they will take pride in having contributed to this book. I could never have completed it without them. I would like to express a special thank you to the following colleagues who were always available for a late-evening phone call or an opinion on the many questions that arose:

Teeda LoCodo, for combining her knowledge of mushrooms with elegant artistry to make this a beautiful book.

Stan Stillman, who recognized the potential market for the cookbook and rescued me from the puzzling intricacies of the publishing business. Without his know-how, this book could not have been published.

Fred Stevens, Ph.D., for writing the section on home cultivation of mushrooms. He assisted in editing the text. He politely answered my many questions on the phone, and never tried to escape when I cornered him at our society meetings.

Harry Thiers, Ph.D., who took time from his busy teaching schedule at San Francisco State University in San Francisco to check the manuscript for scientific and taxonomic accuracy, and who wrote the section on mushroom manners.

Paul Vergeer, for offering his encyclopedic understanding of mushroom toxicology. I appreciate the time he spent verifying that we had not over- or understated remarks about the risks of eating wild mushrooms.

Larry Stickney, for sharing his storehouse of knowledge about mushrooms and their uses in the kitchen. He reviewed the manuscript and offered ideas and recipes.

Francesca Freedman, my daughter, who helped prepare the manuscript for the publisher.

Henry Mee, Ph.D., for making his unique and extensive knowledge of Chinese medicine available to us. For many of us, this is a promising new subject with which to become more acquainted.

Jon Jacobs, for contributing data on the culinary history of mushrooms.

Norene Wedam, a member of the North American Truffling Society, who responded to my call for help in preparing the section on truffles.

Herb Saylor, for supplying material for the truffle section.

Greg Wright, for reviewing the manuscript for technical accuracy.

Diana Kirk, for advice on how to submit material to publishers.

David Largent, Ph.D., for his encouragement and assistance in initiating this project.

Toby Freedman, for assistance in editing the final manuscript.

Roy Halling, Ph.D., for providing information from the New York Botanical Garden concerning East Coast mushrooms.

For supplying foreign mushroom names: Joan Plumb, Finnish; Bea and Stellan Aker, Swedish; Paul Vergeer, German, French, and Dutch; and John Lennie, Russian.

Roma Wagner, for reviewing recipes.

John Garrone from the Farmer's Market in San Francisco, who supplied mushrooms for testing.

Walter and Arline Deitch, for describing their culinary experiences with East Coast mushrooms.

Ann Hart, for providing the list of mushroom societies.

Gene Coleman, John Lennie, Karel Edith for reviewing the galleys.

The following members of the Mycological Society of San Francisco for their continued support: Loraine Berry, president, 1985-86; Leon Ilnicki, vice-president; Karel Edith; Peter Hart; David Moon; members of the MSSF Council for 1985-86.

I especially wish to thank the staff at Aris Books and Carolyn Miller, our proficient editor. I am indebted to John Harris, publisher of Aris Books, for solving many of our problems, and to Karen Hewitt, in-house editor, for her support and understanding.

Finally, Bill Freedman, M.D., my husband, who was always available to add copy, rewrite, and edit every word and page and chapter in this book, and who happily put on ten pounds by bravely volunteering to be stuffed just like my mushrooms. I especially appreciated his analytical approach to each dish I prepared. It would have been difficult to complete this project without him.

Introduction

KITCHEN MAGIC WITH MUSHROOMS, the first cookbook of the Mycological Society of San Francisco, was written in 1962 by the late Charles Sharp. It was very well received, not only by our members, but by other mushroom enthusiasts and professional chefs. In 1980 we decided it was time to write a second book to accommodate changing perspectives and a heightened interest in the preparation of wild and cultivated mushrooms for the table. This gave us the opportunity to check the recipes described in *Kitchen Magic with Mushrooms* for accuracy and to include mushrooms in this book that had been introduced to the public since the publication of the original cookbook.

Recipes were requested and received from members of other groups as well as from our own society members. The remaining recipes are from the author's collection and *Kitchen Magic with Mushrooms.*

The mushrooms presented in this cookbook were selected for their availability and safeness. Most recipes were planned for four servings. It was difficult to be exact in the amounts of mushrooms to be used in the recipes due to the varying sizes, shapes, and degrees of dryness of the mushrooms. Those who use these recipes will have to apply that cookbook judgment alluded to in the phrase "not too much, not too little."

We experimented with many methods of preparation, with wines, and with various flavor enhancers. Our conclusion was that the simplest preparations were the best. We found that it was easy to overwhelm the delicate subtlety of most mushroom flavors. Our primary purpose was to enhance and highlight these qualities.

The most exciting developments in the mushroom world today involve new methods of cultivation and the introduction of new species. As improved techniques are applied commercially, we are witnessing a great expansion in the mushroom industry. Colorful varieties such as the golden-brown butter mushroom, *Pholiota aurivella,* and the red-brown wine-cap mushroom, *Stropharia rugosoannulata,* are starting to appear in produce markets.

Many Asian mushrooms such as the *shiitake* mushroom, once limited to Asian stores, can be purchased in large supermarkets. In the past, we were only able to find Asian mushrooms dried and packaged, but now fresh forms such as *shiitakes* are making their welcome debut. We have learned that these mushrooms are as delicious in stews, casseroles, and sauces as they are in stir-fried dishes. And the cultivation of freshly grown wild mushrooms has been perfected for some varieties, allowing us to have readily accessible and delectable taste treats in our kitchens.

Although this book may introduce the reader to untried and new mushrooms, we hope you will not overlook the tried and true ones. It is not in snobbery, but in praise, that we raise our noses to appreciate the aroma of the common store mushroom. We love and admire it for its generally robust flavor, firm texture, attractive appearance, availability, low cost, and capacity to combine with other foodstuffs, as well as its keeping quality. It pleases us to report that this kitchen Cinderella can be substituted in most of our recipes, and that it will be in season all year long and in any weather.

All living things have been systematically named with two Latinized words. The first word refers to the general group with which the individual shares common characteristics, the *genus*. The second, the *species* name, refers to members of the group according to their individual features. The scientific name for the common store mushroom, for example, is *Agaricus bisporus*. *Agaricus* is the genus and *bisporus* is the species name.

Common names have also been given to many mushrooms, but they vary from country to country and region to region. You can never be sure what kind of mushroom is referred to when someone tells you it's O.K. to eat a "slippery jack." Try to learn the Latin names. Knowing the scientific name will help you identify and discuss mushrooms with others. Try to learn one species at a time. In the long run, scientific names are more useful and less confusing than common names.

PART ONE

A Cook's Introduction to Mushrooms

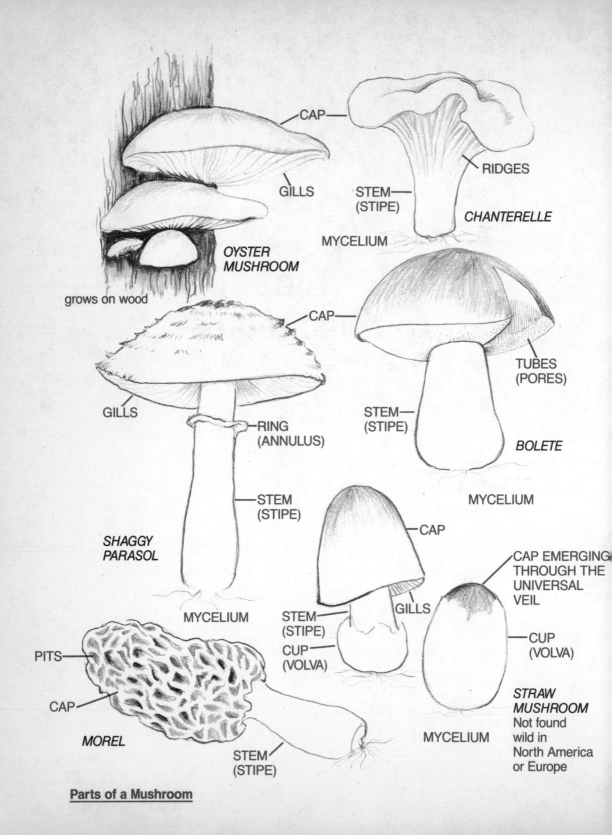

CAP

GILLS

OYSTER MUSHROOM

grows on wood

CAP

RIDGES

STEM (STIPE)

CHANTERELLE

MYCELIUM

CAP

GILLS

RING (ANNULUS)

STEM (STIPE)

SHAGGY PARASOL

MYCELIUM

CAP

TUBES (PORES)

STEM (STIPE)

BOLETE

MYCELIUM

CAP

GILLS

STEM (STIPE)

CUP (VOLVA)

CAP EMERGING THROUGH THE UNIVERSAL VEIL

CUP (VOLVA)

STRAW MUSHROOM
Not found wild in North America or Europe

MYCELIUM

PITS

CAP

MOREL

STEM (STIPE)

Parts of a Mushroom

Cooking with Wild and Cultivated Mushrooms

MUSHROOM LOVERS wait patiently each year for enough rain to fall in fields and forests so they can grab their baskets and take off for their favorite hunting grounds. A new breed of mushroom admirers has learned that they can do their foraging in markets and stores which may feature wild delicacies harvested from distant parts long before local species appear. What's more, the probability of finding them on a single trip to the grocer is much greater than traveling to the woods. So for many wild-mushroom fanciers, it is no longer necessary to foray into lands festooned with poison oak and to risk a wet-footed trip through the forest.

Interest in mushrooms has increased dramatically in the last few years. Food magazines offer tempting recipes for both wild and cultivated mushrooms. Restaurant menus offer such dishes as *porcini* sauce over pasta, or chanterelle quiche. A well-written quarterly magazine dealing solely with fungi is now available. Its contributors are the most active and knowledgeable mushroom enthusiasts in this country. It is called *Mushroom: The Journal of Wild Mushrooming* (see Bibliography).

The potential market is now so great that large-scale cultivation of an increasing variety of fungi provides year-round pleasure for the mushroom fancier.

The use of mushrooms as food has a long and interesting history. The Romans and the Greeks explored the culinary possibilities of fungi with enthusiasm. One mushroom was so highly prized by the Romans that certain cooking pots were set aside and reserved for its exclusive preparation. It was called a *boletaria,* and the genus Boletus shares this common name. Wealthy Romans hired trained collectors to be certain that the mushrooms on which they dined were edible. Animals and slaves were sometimes fed samples of fungi to test their reactions. No systematic method for identifying and naming mushrooms was adopted by the Romans. Nevertheless, we believe some of the varieties we eat today were to be found on banquet menus and in recipes from Roman times.

Today, in some European countries, trained and certified government inspectors will, for a nominal fee, separate edible from inedible fungi.

Handbooks listing names, addresses, and phone numbers of such identifiers in each city are available to the public. Pharmacists in Germany display fresh mushrooms labeled with both common and scientific names.

The search for a simple test to tell if a mushroom is edible continues. The old myths of cooking with a silver coin or spoon, and the Laotian belief that harmful mushrooms make rice turn red have not been substantiated. For a few years, mycologists believed they could detect a poisonous chemical compound found in mushrooms such as *Amanita phalloides,* but subsequent testing of many harmless species produced the same reaction, rendering the test meaningless.

War, poverty, and cultural customs have forced the people of many countries to survive on wild foods for certain periods of time. The Russians claim that forest mushrooms spelled the difference between life and death during many wars when large numbers of people were forced to leave their cities. Wild mushrooms are a permanent part of the cuisine of many countries. People who collect as their forefathers did seldom become ill, because they limit their collections to a small number of well-known fungi.

Wild mushrooms fruit in flushes, reach peak quality for a short time, then vanish until the following year. Frequently, too many are collected to be consumed fresh, and since they are perishable, techniques for preserving them have been devised. They may be dried, pickled, frozen, or canned. Powders are made by grinding them after drying. "Ketchups" are concocted and bottled, and sometimes the mushrooms are salted down, a brining process in which salt is layered with the mushrooms.

In some European countries the number of areas where one can look for wild mushrooms is limited, but the number of foragers is not. Special days have been set aside for collecting in parks, and in some areas there are signs in three languages forbidding mushroom collecting. Research has yet to explain why the numbers of some wild mushrooms have declined in recent years. Some experts speculate that acid rain may be the cause; others feel that poor land management is responsible. The overpicking of wild mushrooms may be a factor and this is being carefully controlled in Europe. Similar concerns have been expressed in the northwestern United States and Canada that fields and forests may be altered or injured from overpicking.

In the United States, local and distant forays to favorite collecting areas are sponsored by mushroom societies. Their equipment is simple. Many people bring baskets or brown paper bags to carry edible varieties. Their baskets are as varied and individual as are their hats. Sometimes their baskets are more interesting than their contents.

Waxed paper is used to wrap unidentifiable mushrooms to keep them in good condition until they can be studied at home. A large knife is

Louise and Bill Freedman

used to remove the entire mushroom from the ground in order to closely examine the base. It is also used to trim and remove debris. A hand lens enables collectors to look for fine details. Some bring a notebook in which to record the specific location of an area where a certain type of mushroom grows. For the artistic, it is an opportunity to record nature on paper. A field guide, especially one dealing with regional species, is essential.

Safety

We expect that those who try these recipes will be rewarded with palates sparkling from their new taste experiences. However, we must interject a note of warning to all of you adventurers who follow the culinary trail through these pages of succulent discovery, for we want you not only to be bold, but to grow old enjoying mushrooms.

Readers should be aware that toxic mushrooms may superficially resemble edible ones. We call these "look-alikes." Only by examining specimens carefully with regard to physical details can we distinguish between edible and poisonous wild mushrooms.

It is worth stressing that each single specimen must be carefully identified as well as checked for general good condition. Don't take chances.

When people consider eating wild mushrooms, they always ask these three questions:

"Are there tests to indicate which mushrooms are edible and which ones are not?" *Answer:* Unfortunately, there are *no* simple tests to determine which ones are safe to eat.

"What's the difference between a mushroom and a toadstool?" *Answer:* The word "toadstool" is an indefinite term referring to poisonous mushrooms. It is not commonly used by experts or knowledgeable amateurs.

"Is it edible?" *Answer:* Fungi are grouped for edibility as follows:

1. Edible and choice.
2. Edible and worth collecting.
3. Harmless, but not worth collecting.
4. Disagreeable.
5. Mildly to severely irritating.
6. Poisonous to lethal.

The mushrooms in which we are interested are limited to the first two groups. But we have learned to know the others so that we can delight in eating edible forms with assurance.

Those who intend to forage in the countryside should review available field guides and publications describing local species and their habitats. Suitable books may be found in college libraries, in bookstores, or in museums dealing with the natural sciences (see Bibliography). Although field guides are helpful in identifying mushrooms, beginners should take their collections to a mushroom expert for proper verification. Contact a mushroom club in your area (see Mycological Societies of the United States and Canada).

Selecting Mushrooms

Whether kneeling happily under a tree collecting golden mushrooms or standing in a produce market weighing them on a scale, you must be able to *identify accurately* any wild mushrooms you plan to eat. Each individual mushroom must be examined to be certain it is the kind you think it is.

Commercial wild-mushroom collectors sell mushrooms to retail outlets. At the present time, anyone may do this, since licenses are not required. Government agencies are in the process of developing guidelines to protect the consumer. Most retailers rely on the judgment of the person who collects the mushrooms to identify them properly. Restaurateurs are sometimes better trained. Ultimately, consumers must take some responsibility in evaluating their purchases and should shop at produce markets where they trust the produce buyer's judgment. It is exciting today to see so many wild mushrooms for sale to the general consumer.

Usually, when we decide to sample a mushroom we've never eaten before, we slice and sauté a small amount of it in butter until it is brown and soft. Then we eat it with plain crackers or toast to evaluate the intensity and the quality of its flavor. These characteristics help us decide how it might be used in a recipe. This procedure will also alert us to any allergic sensitivity we may have to it. Any new food can cause unpleasant minor reactions.

Both wild and cultivated mushrooms should be carefully checked for freshness. Brown, shiny, smelly soft spots will appear if decay has begun. Look for fragmenting gills or pore surfaces, and for worm holes. The cap should be firm and have a wholesome odor.

Examine dried mushrooms sold in plastic bags with care to be sure the mushrooms are not broken or showing other signs of age. They may be stored in clean dry cans or bottles, well sealed to prevent moisture or insects from entering.

Avoid the use of plastic bags for gathering or storing fresh mushrooms. Waxed or brown paper bags are preferred. Water condenses on the walls of plastic, making mushrooms moist or soggy. If they must be carried home from the store in plastic bags, remove them to a dry bowl as soon as possible. If the specimens are very moist, line and cover the bowl with a cloth or paper towel before refrigerating. Most mushrooms will last a week if treated this way.

Cleaning Mushrooms

As a rule, clean mushrooms as you use them. Wash them with as little water as possible. Especially avoid wetting the undersides of the caps. If the mushrooms are in good condition, brush or wipe them with a damp cloth. Delicate flavors are lost in soaking or boiling mushrooms.

Remove tough stems or trim the ends as needed. In some recipes, the stems are saved for later use.

Forest debris and soil can be often persuaded to leave the surface with the gentle brushing of a finger. Nylon mushroom brushes are available at cookware stores, but a soft toothbrush is just as effective.

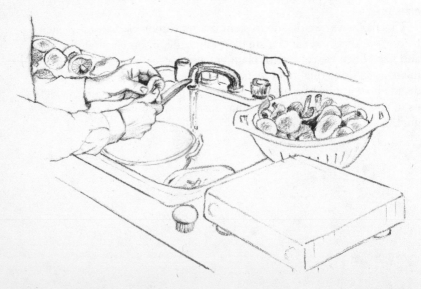

A sharp pointed instrument such as a knife is sometimes required to clean out cracks in chanterelle caps.

In general, mushrooms should be cleaned at least half an hour before cooking so they can dry off. Mary Etta Moose, of the Washington Square Bar and Grill in San Francisco, suggests carefully tossing mushrooms in a dry skillet over heat for a short time to sear their surfaces and to help remove water.

Cooking Tips

Eating Raw Mushrooms: With a few exceptions, such as the common store mushroom, we do not recommend that mushrooms be eaten raw. Uncooked mushroom tissues are poorly broken down for digestion, depriving us of their nutritional contents. Many varieties of wild mushrooms are disagreeable when eaten raw because of viscid surfaces or peppery characteristics. However, they become readily digestible and delectable when cooked.

Using Butter and Cream: Butter seems to enhance the flavor of most mushrooms, except for some of the Asian varieties such as *matsutakes* and the ear mushrooms. We recommend unsalted butter in cooking. Lemon juice helps mushrooms maintain their color and adds zest to their flavor.

It is a common observation that mushrooms in some recipes seem to taste much better when cream is added. It is a culinary reality that cannot be avoided despite the current trend away from cream sauces. Milk may substituted for cream if diet is of greater importance than taste.

Adding Salt: It is recommended that salt be added to most of the recipes in this book to satisfy individual taste preferences. We are aware that many mushroom fanciers must limit salt for health reasons. Salt should be added towards the end of cooking, since it tends to remove water from mushroom tissues and makes them too soft.

Slicing Mushrooms: Slicing mushrooms allows for more rapid cooking and water loss than when mushrooms are cooked whole. Cut them into uniform thicknesses and they will cook more evenly. Mushrooms with mild and subtle flavors should be cut into large pieces so that their savory juices can be better appreciated. The best tool for cutting mushrooms is a sharp 5¼-inch utility knife.

For uniform slicing, because the caps have varying sizes, shapes, and textures, cut mushrooms in half so that they will lie flat on the surface of the cutting board. Soft species such as shaggy manes are difficult to cut unless the knife is sharp and the cut firm.

Precooking Mushrooms: Wild mushrooms are often precooked, for several different reasons. If freezer storage is planned, it is best to sauté them in butter first, so they will have firmer texture when used later. Making *duxelles* is another way of preparing a mushroom in advance and utilizing otherwise discarded portions of mushrooms. To prepare marinated mushrooms, either parboil them or simmer them in the marinade liquid. Vinegar and other acidic combinations do not have the same chemical action as does heat and will not eliminate toxins. Certain helvella mushrooms should be parboiled to remove toxins and the water discarded before adding the mushrooms to other ingredients.

Using Dried Mushrooms: In using dried mushrooms, first rinse them quickly under the faucet and then place them in a bowl. Pour enough hot water over them to cover and soak for the recommended period of time for each type of mushroom. Soaking time will vary because of the different size, thickness, and shape of each variety. As a rule, this should take at least 15 to 20 minutes. Remove the mushrooms and squeeze them dry. Save the soaking liquid for use in your recipe since much mushroom flavor will have been released while rehydrating. Decant the soaking liquid slowly to avoid adding sediment that has settled to the bottom of the vessel.

Intensifying Flavor: Mushrooms exude liquid when sautéed in oil or butter. Many chefs prefer to cook most of the fluid off to develop the maximum intensity of the mushroom's flavor. Some recipes require browning the mushrooms to create more flavor. While doing this, constant vigilance is required to avoid burning.

Preserving Mushrooms

There are four excellent reasons for preserving mushrooms:

1. They are very seasonal. Wild mushrooms are sold in the markets cyclically at the same time as they appear in their natural habitats. We must enjoy them fresh while we can. As a rule, they are most tasty when

fresh. But many varieties, if carefully preserved, can be coaxed to hold on to their flavors for later use.

2. Mushroom prices are at their lowest when they are being harvested in quantity. This lasts for a few weeks or months, depending on the species. If you are lucky enough to find or to inexpensively buy a large quantity at one time, it may be impossible to cook and eat all of them. There are two options to be explored: either give the excess away to friends, or preserve them for later use.

3. Fungi do not keep well for long. After eating and enjoying some for a few days, holding the rest increases the risk of spoiling. To make the most of the leftover mushrooms, it is wise to safely put the remainder away until your taste buds again urge you to repeat past pleasures.

4. Transporting fresh fungi is difficult. They break and bruise easily. They do not tolerate exposure well. Therefore they can be merchandised by drying, canning, freezing, grinding, pickling, or as ketchup.

Drying Mushrooms

One of the earliest methods of preserving food was to dry it. This is still an effective way to keep mushrooms for a long time without spoiling. Their taste will usually be altered in the process. Sometimes the flavor becomes more intense, and sometimes their original qualities are lost. Some varieties of mushrooms take on nuances not found when fresh. Begin by selecting mushrooms that are in good condition. They should be firm, without many worm holes, and capable of withstanding gentle handling.

When cleaning, try to prevent the mushroom from taking on water, which is what we want to get rid of. The underside of the cap is particularly prone to holding onto liquid. Clean the top of the cap with a brush, a damp cloth, or your finger. Trim the stems.

Cut flat, even, broad slices about ⅜-inch thick. The slices should be of uniform width so that they will dry at the same speed. Plan to work on your mushrooms as soon as you bring them home. Do not leave them lying around to deteriorate. Avoid overlapping the slices on trays so that they will dry evenly.

Many mushroom fanciers have developed unique drying techniques. Some hang flats of wire screen doors, plastic mesh, etc., overhead with wire or cord, especially above ovens, fireplaces, or heating units. One creative person has converted an abandoned refrigerator into an efficient dryer using a fan and a 75-watt light bulb. Many effective and inexpensive commercial dehydrators are available.

When slices are *bone dry*, no less, place in metal cans or glass jars. If you are uncertain about their state of dryness, transfer them into paper bags, and hang in a dry, warm place over an oven or fireplace for a few days. Then put them into containers, adding a few dried bay leaves or a handful of whole black peppers to discourage insect pests. Be sure to label containers with the date and the species identification.

Freezing Mushrooms

Freezing is a fine technique for putting mushrooms away for a future day when none are growing. They can be frozen fresh or precooked. Some small caps may be frozen whole, after examining, cleaning, and completely draining them. Allow 20 to 30 minutes for draining. Larger specimens should be sliced or cubed into ¼-inch pieces. Heavy plastic is acceptable for freezing, or use freezing containers. *Matsutakes* and the boletes are preserved beautifully this way, retaining their aromas and spiciness as well as their textures.

There are two methods of precooking mushrooms for freezing. One way is simply to freeze a dish made with mushrooms, such as a quiche, ready to heat and serve. The other is to sauté the mushrooms in butter or oil, or both, for 5 minutes before transferring them to a freezer container. Be sure to include the liquid remaining in your saucepan. Such food will keep well for 6 months.

Stuffed Mushrooms

It's easy to develop a mutual admiration relationship with mushrooms. You stuff them, then let them stuff you. Common store mushrooms are perfect receptacles for a variety of foodstuffs such as onions, tomatoes, greens, meat, or chopped mushroom stems enhanced with butter, herbs, or spices.

The simplest mode of preparation is to remove the stem from the cap or use hollow-capped species such as morels. Stuff them, and bake. They don't last long as party food, and they will contribute complements and compliments for your main course at dinner.

Use medium- to large-sized caps: medium for hors d'oeuvres and appetizers, large ones for main dishes. Select very firm mushrooms with broad stems and unopened caps that will hold more stuffing.

Clean the tops and stems with a soft brush and a little water. Drain for 15 to 30 minutes in a colander. Remove any debris from the stems, and freshen up the cut end of the stem by trimming.

Gently twist off the stems of gilled mushrooms. You may need to use the end of a knife to encourage the stem to leave. Remove the cottony veil from common store mushrooms and their relatives. Don't fail to incorporate these fragments and the stems in the stuffing.

Prepare the caps by brushing them with soft or melted butter. This will sear the surface of the mushroom when heated and will help it hold its shape. Another way of firming up caps is to brush them with butter and broil them cavity-side down under a preheated broiler for 5 minutes before being filled.

Stuffing material should be partially or completely precooked and ready for placement as soon as the caps have been prepared. Spoon the stuffing into the hollowed portion of the caps, press the material down tightly, and move the caps onto your baking surface. Mushrooms release a good deal of liquid when heated, so it is best to use a shallow baking pan or a jelly roll pan, which has raised edges, to retain the juices. It is advisable to fill them before placing them on the baking pan, since you want your mushrooms to have a neat appearance. And the pan will be much easier to clean.

Baking or broiling time will vary according to the size of the cap and the nature of the filling. It is best to start with a preheated oven. Keep your eye on your achievements, allowing them to brown without burning. Serve them immediately.

Mushroom varieties other than the common store ones may be stuffed, such as:

Boletus edulis (*cèpes* or *porcini*): Large caps may be prepared as small pizzas. Serve stuffed boletes alongside your meat or fish dish; they may be filled with a wide variety of foods appropriate to the entrée. The superb full flavor of this mushroom's juice blends with any stuffing to make it unique and rich.

Agaricus augustus (the prince): One of the best mushrooms for stuffing because it is usually large and the cap forms a deep bowl. The strong, sweet almond flavor exuding from the prince adds an exotic quality to whatever ingredients you select to stuff it with, such as sautéed chopped stems cooked with minced garlic, bread crumbs, fresh tomatoes, and soy sauce. The special princely flavor filters through all the ingredients.

Morels: These were designed by nature for stuffing. Fill their hollow interiors with mixtures of ground beef, bacon, lamb, crab, or simply browned onions, bread crumbs, and parsley. Any stuffing will feature the morel's fabulous aftertaste.

Shiitakes: This is the finest of the cultivated mushrooms. Asian recipes frequently recommend steaming them when they are filled. Dry *shiitakes* should be reconstituted for 20 minutes in hot water before using.

Matsutakes: Expensive to buy and rare to find, a large stuffed *matsutake* could be the vegetable for a large dinner party. You might want to marinate it with soy sauce and dry sherry for 20 minutes. Remove the stem and use it chopped with pork or chicken, moistened with the marinade. Brush the cap with peanut oil. Fill and grill or bake in a hot oven until brown. Small *matsutakes* can be stuffed by making a cut in the cap and spreading the opening enough to place stuffing inside. They are very attractive served with steamed vegetables.

You will find suggestions for other stuffing mixtures in the sections on specific mushrooms.

Quick Reference Chart

This chart will help you select ways to use wild and cultivated mushrooms.

	Black Chanterelle	Black Saddle	Blewit	Boletes	Candy Cap	Chanterelle	Common Store	Ear Mushrooms	Enoki	Fairy Ring Mushroom	Hedgehog Mushroom	Honey Mushroom	Matsutake	Milky Caps	Morels	Nameko	Oyster Mushroom	Puffballs	Shaggy Mane	Shaggy Parasol	Shiitake	Snow Mushroom	Straw Mushroom	Truffles
Baking		•		•		•	•				•			•			•	•	•				•	
Beef		•		•							•	•	•	•			•	•			•		•	
Bisques						•									•			•						
Breads				•	•	•	•			•														
Broiling				•			•														•		•	
Canning		•	•	•		•	•	•	•	•	•	•		•		•	•				•	•	•	•
Cheese	•		•	•		•	•							•			•				•			
Chowders	•		•	•			•				•	•		•			•							
Chutneys	•		•		•		•	•				•		•										
Clay-pot cooking		•					•							•							•	•		
Crêpes	•	•		•		•	•							•	•		•		•	•	•			•
Deep-frying		•		•			•							•			•	•	•					
Desserts			•		•						•		•									•		
Drying	•	•		•		•		•													•	•	•	
Duxelles	•		•	•		•		•																
Eggs	•	•	•	•		•	•			•	•			•							•		•	
Fish		•	•	•		•	•					•	•	•			•				•		•	
Freezing	•	•	•	•		•	•			•	•			•			•	•	•		•		•	
Grains	•	•	•	•		•	•	•		•				•							•			
Grilling				•									•	•			•				•	•	•	
Ham & bacon				•	•		•				•		•											
Lamb				•			•											•						
Marinating		•	•	•		•	•				•	•		•	•									
Omelettes	•	•	•	•		•	•		•					•			•	•		•	•		•	
Pastas	•		•			•	•				•		•				•				•		•	
Pastries			•		•		•			•				•							•			
Pâtés	•			•		•	•																	•
Pickling		•	•	•	•	•	•																	
Pizzas	•	•	•			•	•																	
Poultry	•	•	•	•		•	•				•		•				•		•		•		•	
Pork		•				•	•				•	•		•									•	
Powdered	•			•	•		•										•				•			
Quiches			•	•		•	•				•						•				•			
Raw							•	•	•				•			•								
Relishes				•			•			•		•				•	•							
Salads	•				•		•			•	•						•							
Sauces	•	•		•		•	•				•		•		•		•		•		•			
Sautéing	•	•	•	•		•	•			•	•	•		•			•		•		•	•		•
Shellfish				•		•	•	•	•												•			
Soufflé				•			•			•				•							•		•	
Soups			•	•	•	•	•	•	•	•			•				•				•	•		
Steaming						•	•					•					•				•			
Stewing		•		•		•	•					•									•			
Stir-frying			•			•	•	•				•	•				•				•		•	
Strudels	•		•			•	•																•	•
Stuffed		•		•			•								•					•	•			•
Stuffings	•	•		•		•	•							•						•	•			
Sweetbreads	•			•		•	•							•			•				•			
Tofu	•					•	•						•				•	•			•		•	
Veal		•		•		•	•				•							•			•			•
Vegetables	•	•	•	•		•	•			•		•		•			•				•		•	•

PART TWO

Basic Mushroom Recipes

THIS SECTION is devoted to recipes in which a variety of mushrooms may be used. Each mushroom has its own unique qualities and will make distinctive dishes with the most basic recipes. The blandness of rice, for instance, can be enhanced by many different types of mushrooms. Please take advantage of the suggested alternate mushrooms that can be substituted in these recipes, but feel free to use any mushroom available in your produce market.

Duxelles

Makes 1 cup

This is a good way to store perishable mushrooms for future use in sauces, stuffings, and as a flavoring agent for soups and casseroles. Use the stems from stuffed mushrooms to make *duxelles,* and save the mushroom juices to add to soups and other dishes. *Duxelles* can be covered and stored in the refrigerator for at least 1 week.

Alternate Mushrooms:
blewit, boletes, common store mushroom

1 pound mushrooms, minced
1 small onion, minced
2 shallots or green onions,
  minced
4 tablespoons butter
1 teaspoon fresh lemon juice
Salt and pepper to taste
Pinch of grated nutmeg

Place the minced mushrooms in the center of a cotton tea towel. Twist the ends of the towel to squeeze as much liquid from the mushrooms as possible, collecting the juices in a bowl. Save the juice for another dish.

In a sauté pan or skillet, sauté the mushrooms, onion, and shallots in the butter until the onion is translucent. Add the lemon juice, salt, pepper, and nutmeg. Continue to cook, stirring, until nearly all the moisture is evaporated. —Kitchen Magic with Mushrooms

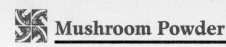
Mushroom Powder

Makes 1 cup

Mushrooms can be ground to a powder when thoroughly dried. Each variety will impart different flavors to sauces, soups, broiled fish, meat, and chicken. Puffballs are especially favored when used in this manner. Mushroom powder will keep for 4 to 6 months.

Alternate Mushrooms:
boletes, black chanterelle, puffballs, shaggy parasol mushroom

3 to 4 pounds mushrooms, cut into ¼-inch slices
1 teaspoon salt
1 teaspoon ground black pepper
Few grains of cayenne
2 teaspoons cornstarch, to prevent caking (optional)

Dry the mushroom slices (see page 11). When the slices are nearly dry, remove in 2 to 3 batches to baking sheets. Place in a preheated 300° oven and toast until golden brown.

After the slices have cooled, place a few at a time in a blender or a food processor and blend to a fine powder. Repeat this procedure until all the mushrooms have been pulverized. Add the other ingredients and blend.

Store in a glass container with a tightly closed top.   —Kitchen Magic with Mushrooms

Mushroom Relish

Makes 3 pints

An unusual relish that can be served with beef ribs, hamburgers, chuck roast, or mild-flavored fish.

Alternate Mushrooms:
blewit, common store mushroom, puffballs

4 pounds mushrooms, coarsely chopped
2 green bell peppers, seeded and coarsely chopped
1 red bell pepper, seeded and coarsely chopped
2 tablespoons salt
4 whole cloves
1 teaspoon peppercorns
1 teaspoon whole allspice berries
2 teaspoons mustard seeds
1 cup wine vinegar
1 cup sugar

In a large mixing bowl, combine the mushrooms, green peppers, and red pepper. Add the salt and mix well. Weigh down with a plate that fits inside the bowl. Place a heavy object on top, such as a stone. Let it stand overnight.

Place the spices in a cheesecloth bag. Tie securely with cotton string.

Combine the vinegar, sugar, and spice bag in a large heavy pot and bring to a boil. Squeeze the liquid out of the mushroom mixture with your hands and place the mushrooms in the pot. Simmer for 15 minutes.

With a slotted spoon, pack mushrooms firmly in hot sterilized pint jars. Remove excess liquid and seal. Process 20 minutes in a canner.　　　　　　　*—Louise Freedman*

Mushroom Chutney

Makes 2 pint jars

Sweet and spicy mushrooms and tart apples combine to liven up beef, ham, and poultry.

Alternate Mushrooms:
common store mushroom, puffballs

2 pounds mushrooms, sliced
2 tart apples, peeled, pared, and
   chopped
1 onion, chopped
½ cup raisins
2 tablespoons grated fresh ginger
¾ cup brown sugar or more
¼ teaspoon ground cloves
¼ teaspoon ground cinnamon
⅛ teaspoon freshly ground
   nutmeg
½ cup distilled white vinegar
1 teaspoon salt

Place all the ingredients in a large saucepan and cook slowly, uncovered, for 45 minutes to 1 hour or until most of the liquid has evaporated. Pack into hot sterilized jars and process in a canner for 5 minutes.
   —*Tom Flynn, from* Rocky Mountain
   Mushroom Cookbook

Mushroom Ketchup

Makes 2 pint jars

An unusual relish that goes well
with hamburgers, corned beef,
and cheese or cold meat
sandwiches.

Alternate Mushrooms:
common store mushroom, fairy
ring mushroom

2 pounds mushrooms, drained
    and trimmed
One ¼-inch slice fresh ginger,
    peeled and minced
5 garlic cloves, minced
½ cup white distilled vinegar
One 8-ounce can tomato sauce
½ teaspoon ground allspice
½ teaspoon ground cloves
1 teaspoon sugar
1½ teaspoons salt or more

Puree the mushrooms, ginger, and garlic in
small amounts in a blender or food processor
until the mixture becomes pastelike. Place it in
a heavy pot. Add the remaining ingredients
and simmer uncovered for 1 hour, stirring
occasionally. Pack into hot sterilized jars.
Process in a canner for 15 minutes.

—*Louise Freedman*

Mushroom-Cream Sauce

Makes 1 cup

A basic sauce especially designed for dried mushrooms, although small fresh caps may be used. Preparation time is short, since the dried caps are rehydrated in the cooking process. Excellent over pasta, chicken breasts, veal, and hot buttered toast.

Alternate Mushrooms:
black chanterelle, boletes, fairy ring mushroom, morels

1½ ounces dried mushrooms, or
   ½ pound fresh small
   mushrooms
3 tablespoons butter
2 tablespoons water or more
1 cup half and half
Salt to taste
Pinch of white pepper
3 tablespoons water
1 tablespoon flour

If using dried mushrooms, quickly run water over the mushrooms in a colander to remove any sand just before cooking.

In a medium-sized saucepan, melt the butter and add the water. Add the mushrooms and cook slowly (for about 3 minutes) until the caps are soft. Add more water if needed. Add the half and half, salt, and white pepper. Simmer for 3 to 5 minutes. Blend the water and flour together and slowly stir into the sauce. Cook and stir 5 minutes until the sauce thickens.　—Kitchen Magic with Mushrooms

Tomato-Mushroom Sauce

Makes 4 cups

An elegant tomato sauce easily prepared in advance and stored in the refrigerator. Spoon it over freshly cooked and drained ravioli or pasta. Sprinkle with Romano or Parmesan cheese. This sauce is especially good with boletes, chanterelles, or common store mushrooms.

1 pound fresh mushrooms, or
   3 ounces dried mushrooms
4 garlic cloves, chopped
2 tablespoons olive oil
1 pound ground turkey or beef
1 teaspoon chopped fresh mint
   leaves (optional)
½ teaspoon dried rosemary
¼ teaspoon dried oregano
¼ teaspoon dried thyme
One 15-ounce can tomato sauce
Salt and pepper to taste
½ cup dry red wine or more

If using fresh mushrooms, cut into chunks; if using dried ones, soak them in hot water to cover for about 15 minutes, squeeze dry, and chop. Save the soaking liquid for the sauce.

In a large sauté pan or skillet, sauté the mushrooms and garlic for 7 minutes in the olive oil. Remove the mushrooms and garlic with a slotted spoon. Add the turkey or beef and cook for another 3 minutes, crumbling the meat as it cooks. Add the mint, rosemary, oregano, thyme, tomato sauce, salt, pepper, red wine, mushroom-garlic mixture, and the soaking liquid from the dried mushrooms if you have it. Cover and simmer for 1 hour. If you want a richer flavor, add more wine during the last 10 minutes of cooking.

—*Peggy Sanders*

Mushroom Velouté Sauce

Makes about 2½ cups

A classic sauce to be used with most mushrooms. Excellent over sweetbreads, fish, or poultry.

½ pound fresh young
   mushrooms
4 tablespoons butter
2 shallots or green onions,
   chopped
2 tablespoons flour
1 cup rich milk, scalded
1 cup chicken broth
Few grains of nutmeg
Salt and pepper to taste

In a sauté pan or skillet, sauté the mushrooms in 2 tablespoons of the butter for 3 to 4 minutes, adding the shallots the last few minutes. In a saucepan, melt the remaining 2 tablespoons of butter and stir in the flour. Cook and stir for 2 to 3 minutes. Whisk in the milk and broth. Simmer over very low heat, whisking often, until the sauce is thickened. Add the mushrooms, nutmeg, salt, and pepper.

—Kitchen Magic with Mushrooms

Mushroom Mayonnaise

Makes 2 cups

An excellent salad dressing. Spread on bread or toast or add to sandwiches. This mayonnaise will keep in the refrigerator for several days.

Alternate Mushrooms:
common store mushroom, black chanterelle

2 eggs, at room temperature
1 teaspoon salt
1 teaspoon Dijon-style mustard, or ½ teaspoon dry mustard
2 tablespoons fresh lemon juice
1 teaspoon sherry wine vinegar
1 cup mild-flavored vegetable oil
¼ pound mushrooms

Combine the eggs, salt, and mustard in a food processor or blender and blend for 10 seconds. Add the lemon juice and vinegar and blend for 10 more seconds. Add the oil in a slow stream, together with the mushrooms, one at a time. Refrigerate. *—Tom Flynn, from* Rocky Mountain Mushroom Cookbook

Mushrooms à la Grecque

Serves 12 as an appetizer

There are never leftovers when these succulent appetizers are served. Guests usually soak up the sauce with French bread. These mushrooms are also delectable tossed with a salad.

Alternate Mushrooms:
common store mushroom, meadow mushroom

1 pound small button
   mushrooms
⅓ cup olive oil
3 tablespoons balsamic vinegar
2 garlic cloves, minced
½ teaspoon salt
2 tablespoons brandy
½ teaspoon ground pepper
2 tablespoons chopped fresh
   parsley
½ teaspoon each minced fresh
   thyme and oregano, or
   ⅛ teaspoon each dried thyme
   and oregano

Place all the ingredients in a saucepan and simmer very slowly for 10 minutes. Mix gently a few times. Allow the mushrooms to cool in the liquid. Drain and serve with toothpicks.
   —Kitchen Magic with Mushrooms

Marinated Mushrooms with Onion Rings

Serves 12 as an appetizer

These mushrooms will keep in the refrigerator for 2 weeks. An excellent recipe if you have a pressure cooker for canning. Especially good for chanterelles.

Alternate Mushrooms:
chanterelle, common store mushroom, milky caps, hedgehog mushroom

1 small onion, sliced crosswise
⅓ cup dry red wine
⅓ cup olive oil
¼ cup minced fresh parsley
1 teaspoon Dijon mustard
1 tablespoon light brown sugar
1 teaspoon salt
1 pound mushrooms, thinly
   sliced

Separate the onion into rings. Place all the ingredients except the mushrooms in a large saucepan and bring to a boil. Add the mushrooms and simmer 5 to 6 minutes. Chill in a covered bowl for several hours, stirring a few times.   *—Sally Fulton*

Mushrooms Trifolati

Serves 3 to 4 as an appetizer

The powerful anchovy taste requires the presence of a strongly flavored mushroom for balance, such as the shaggy parasol or common store mushroom. Serve on hot toast.

2 tablespoons olive oil
1 garlic clove, chopped
1 pound mushrooms, sliced
1 tablespoon butter
3 anchovy fillets, chopped
Pepper to taste
Juice of ½ lemon
Freshly toasted bread squares
1 teaspoon chopped fresh
   parsley

In a sauté pan or skillet, heat the oil and cook the garlic until translucent. Add the mushrooms and cook for 5 minutes or until all the liquid has evaporated. Add the butter, anchovies, pepper, and lemon juice and cook for 5 minutes. Remove from the heat and serve on squares of toast, sprinkled with the parsley.
   —Kitchen Magic with Mushrooms

Mushroom and Pecan Pâté

Serves 10 at a party

The combination of mushrooms and pecans is outstanding. This pâté is delectable served hot with a creamed mushroom sauce.

1½ pounds mushrooms, chopped (you may use a combination of several varieties, for example: 1 pound common store mushrooms and ½ pound chanterelles or 1 to 2 ounces dried Italian boletes, or *porcini*)

1 onion, minced

½ cup (1 stick) butter

½ teaspoon salt

1 thyme sprig, chopped, or ¼ teaspoon dried thyme

8 eggs, slightly beaten

1 cup grated Emmenthaler cheese

1 cup ground pecans

If you use dried mushrooms, soak them for about 15 minutes in hot water to cover, then drain and squeeze dry. Reserve the soaking liquid.

Cook the onion in the butter over low heat in a heavy pot until the onion is soft. Add the mushrooms, salt, and thyme. Cover and raise the heat for a few minutes. Empty into a strainer and press out as much juice as possible. Reserve the juice. Allow the mushrooms to cool, then mix them with the eggs, cheese, and pecans. Taste for salt and correct seasoning.

Pack the mixture into a buttered loaf pan and cover with foil. Place the loaf pan in a larger pan and pour boiling water into the pan so that it comes halfway up the side of the loaf pan. Bake in a preheated 325° oven for 1 hour or until the pâté is firm and slightly puffed. Allow it to set for 20 minutes before serving.

You can serve this with the mushroom cream sauce on page 21.   —*Paul Johnston*

Mushrooms with Crab Meat

Serves 4 or more as an appetizer

Shellfish blend beautifully as stuffings for mushrooms and crêpes. Scallops, lobster, mussels, and others can be substituted for crab meat.

Alternate Mushrooms:
common store mushroom, horse mushroom, meadow mushroom, morels, the prince

12 to 16 large mushrooms, stems removed
6 tablespoons butter, melted
¾ pound fresh cooked crab meat
2 eggs, beaten
3 tablespoons mayonnaise
¼ cup chopped green onions
2 teaspoons fresh lemon juice
½ cup fresh bread crumbs

Dip the mushroom caps in the melted butter and place them upside down in a buttered baking dish. Save the stems for another meal.

Combine the crab meat, eggs, mayonnaise, onions, lemon juice, and half of the bread crumbs. Fill the mushroom caps with this mixture. Sprinkle the remaining crumbs (and any butter left from dipping the caps) on top of the stuffed caps. Bake in a preheated 375° oven for 15 minutes or until the bread crumbs are golden brown.

—Kitchen Magic with Mushrooms

Mushrooms Florentine

Serves 6 as an appetizer

An attractive and delicious centerpiece for a party.

Alternate Mushrooms:
common store mushroom, horse mushroom, meadow mushroom

½ cup (1 stick) butter
12 large mushrooms, stems
   removed and reserved
1½ tablespoons onion, minced
1 garlic clove, minced
¾ cup cooked spinach, puréed
½ cup ground turkey or pork
¼ teaspoon ground nutmeg
Salt and pepper to taste
2 tablespoons freshly grated
   Parmesan
12 to 16 toasted bread rounds
   (optional)

Melt 6 tablespoons of the butter. Dip the mushroom caps into the melted butter and place them upside down in a buttered baking dish. Chop the mushroom stems and set aside. In a sauté pan or skillet, melt the remaining 2 tablespoons of butter and sauté the onion, garlic and mushroom stems for about 5 minutes. Add the spinach, turkey, nutmeg, salt, and pepper, and cook until the meat is done.

Fill the mushroom caps with the mixture, sprinkle with Parmesan cheese, and bake for 15 minutes or until browned. Serve hot on toasted bread rounds, if desired.

—Kitchen Magic with Mushrooms

Mushrooms Escargot Style

Serves 6 as an appetizer

Dip slices of French bread into the cooking liquid released from these juicy stuffed mushrooms.

Alternate Mushrooms:
common store mushroom, meadow mushroom, the prince

1 tablespoon butter, melted
Few drops fresh lemon juice
1 to 1½ pounds large
    mushrooms, stemmed
2 garlic cloves, minced
½ cup (1 stick) soft butter
2 shallots or green onions,
    minced
½ cup chopped fresh parsley
¼ cup freshly grated Parmesan
    cheese
Salt and pepper
1 loaf sourdough French bread

Combine the melted butter and lemon juice. Rub each mushroom with this mixture. Combine the garlic, soft butter, shallots, parsley, and Parmesan cheese. Add salt and pepper to taste and fill the mushroom cavities. Set in a shallow baking pan and bake in a preheated 400° oven for 10 to 12 minutes.

Serve with slices of French bread to soak up the juices, or set the mushrooms on the bread with toothpicks.   *—Roma M. Wagner*

Stuffed Mushroom Caps

Serves 5 to 6 as an appetizer

A quickly prepared and attractive appetizer made from readily available ingredients.

Alternate Mushrooms:
common store mushroom, meadow mushroom, the prince

1 pound mushrooms
3 tablespoons freshly grated
    Parmesan cheese
2 garlic cloves, minced
1 large onion, minced
1 cup fine bread crumbs
1 tablespoon chopped fresh
    parsley
2 tablespoons butter, melted
Salt and pepper to taste
6 tablespoons olive oil

Remove the stems from the mushrooms; mince the stems. Mix the Parmesan cheese, garlic, onion, bread crumbs, parsley, and melted butter thoroughly. Add the chopped mushroom stems. Season with salt and pepper.

Stuff the caps with the filling. Place 2 tablespoons of the olive oil in a shallow baking pan. Place the stuffed caps in the pan and drizzle the remaining olive oil over the tops of the mushrooms.

Bake in a preheated 400° oven for 25 minutes or until brown and crisp.

—*Alice Desjardin*

Stuffed Mushrooms Lucchese

Serves 4 to 6 as an appetizer or side dish

Large meaty mushrooms are filled with a combination of walnuts and bacon and served as an appetizer or side dish.

Alternate Mushrooms:
common store mushroom, horse mushroom, meadow mushroom, morels, the prince

1½ pounds large mushooms
4 tablespoons butter
1 medium onion, minced
1 cup soft white bread crumbs
1 cup chopped walnuts
1 tablespoon tomato paste
2 tablespoons fresh lemon juice
Salt and pepper to taste
3 bacon strips, cooked, drained, and crumbled
½ cup half and half

Remove the stems from the mushrooms and mince the stems. Melt the butter in a sauté pan or skillet and sauté the onion and stems for 4 minutes. Stir in the bread crumbs, nuts, tomato paste, lemon juice, salt, and pepper and cook for 2 minutes. Let the mixture cool slightly, then stuff the caps. Top with the bacon and bake in a preheated 400° oven for 25 minutes. Remove from the oven. Pour the cream over the mushrooms and bake for 5 more minutes. Serve warm. —*Rose C. Gaspari*

Mushroom Soup with Sherry

Serves 4 as a first course

This recipe originally called for the horse mushroom, a large field mushroom sometimes the size of a dinner plate. Common store mushrooms, *shiitakes,* chanterelles, or milky caps will make an equally delicious soup.

2 tablespoons butter
1 pound mushrooms, chopped
1 large garlic clove, chopped
3 to 4 green onions, chopped
4 cups chicken broth or more
½ cup cooked rice
Salt and pepper to taste
Chopped fresh parsley
4 tablespoons dry sherry

In a sauté pan or skillet, melt the butter and sauté the mushrooms, garlic, and green onions. Cook until most of the liquid has evaporated. Reserve about one-third of the sauté mixture and purée the remainder in a blender or a food processor with about 1 cup of the broth and the rice. The rice stabilizes the soup. Heat the purée in a heavy stockpot; add the remaining broth. Add salt and pepper and the mushrooms. If too thick, add more broth. Garnish with parsley, and at the table have each guest add a tablespoon of sherry to his or her serving. —*Mary Keehner*

Cream of Mushroom Soup

Serves 4 as a first course

A basic cream soup that will highlight the flavor of most kinds of mushrooms.

5 tablespoons butter
1 large onion, chopped into
    small pieces
1½ pounds mushrooms,
    chopped into small pieces
½ cup dry white wine
2½ cups chicken broth
1 cup half and half
Dash of ground nutmeg
Salt and pepper to taste

In a large saucepan, melt the butter and sauté the onion until translucent. Add the mushrooms and continue to sauté for 5 minutes. Stir in the wine and cook for a few minutes, then add the broth. Cook for 15 minutes. Slowly add the half and half and simmer for 5 minutes, never allowing it to boil. When you are ready to serve, add the nutmeg, salt, and pepper. Serve hot. —*Louise Freedman*

Mushroom-Yogurt Soup

Serves 4 to 5 as a first course

A hearty soup once served after a mushroom foray at a College of the Redwoods biology class in Mendocino, California. A green salad and a thick slice of whole-wheat bread covered with goat cheese made the meal complete.

Alternate Mushrooms:
boletes, chanterelle, common store mushroom, shaggy mane

4 tablespoons butter
1 medium onion, chopped
6 green onions, chopped
¾ pound mushrooms, sliced
2 teaspoons paprika
¼ cup flour
6 cups chicken broth
2 egg yolks
1½ cups plain yogurt
1 teaspoon chopped fresh dill, or
    ¼ teaspoon dried dill
Salt and pepper to taste

In a large saucepan, melt the butter and sauté the onions until translucent. Add the mushrooms and cook until soft. Gradually stir in the paprika and flour. Add the broth. Cook, stirring, until thickened. Cover and simmer for 30 minutes.

Lightly beat together the egg yolks, yogurt, and dill. Stir about 1 cup of the hot soup into the egg mixture. Return it to the soup and cook, stirring over very low heat just until it thickens. Do not allow it to boil. Season with salt and pepper.   —Gathered Mushroom Recipes, *College of the Redwoods*

Consommé with Mushrooms

Serves 4 to 6 as a main course

A rich consommé containing a combination of flavors. Serve some mushrooms and capers in each bowl. Toasted garlic-tarragon bread complements this soup.

Alternate Mushrooms:
boletes, common store mushroom

Six 10½-ounce cans beef
   consommé, with an equal
   amount of cold water
1 pound round steak, cubed
3 large leeks, coarsely chopped
1 lemon, sliced without peeling
   into ¼-inch slices
2 medium carrots, quartered and
   cut into 2-inch slices
2 celery stalks, coarsely chopped
2 garlic cloves, crushed
1 bay leaf
2 egg whites
¼ pound fresh mushrooms, cut
   into thin slices
2 tablespoons butter
2 tablespoons fresh lemon juice
2 tablespoons capers, drained
¼ cup brandy
Salt and pepper to taste

Heat the consommé and water in a large soup pot. Add the cubed round steak and bring to a boil. Reduce to a simmer and remove the scum. Add the leeks, lemon slices, carrots, celery, garlic, and bay leaf. Simmer for 2 hours. Remove from the heat and strain the stock. Allow it to cool. Discard the bay leaf.

Beat the egg whites lightly. Add them to the cooled stock and heat, stirring constantly. Strain the stock again, this time through a strainer lined with moistened muslin. The stock should be clear and a rich amber in color.

Sauté the mushrooms in the butter for 2 to 3 minutes, then add the lemon juice and capers. Bring the clarified consommé to a boil. Add the brandy and the salt and pepper to taste. Reduce the heat. Add the mushrooms and capers. Simmer for a few minutes.

Serve portions of mushrooms and capers in each soup plate.

—Kitchen Magic with Mushrooms

Eggs Stuffed with Duxelles

Serves 6 as an appetizer

Duxelles add interest to stuffed eggs. Blewits are particularly impressive prepared in this manner.

Alternate Mushrooms:
boletes, common store mushroom

6 hard-cooked eggs
¼ cup *duxelles* (see page 16)
1 tablespoon mayonnaise
¼ teaspoon Dijon mustard
Salt and pepper
Chopped fresh parsley

Cut the eggs in half lengthwise. Remove the yolks and mash them in a mixing bowl. Blend in the *duxelles,* mayonnaise, mustard, salt, and pepper. Mound the yolk mixture into the egg whites and sprinkle the parsley over the top.

—*Louise Freedman*

Mushroom Frittata

*Serves 4 to 6 as an appetizer or
3 or 4 as a main course*

A flavorful cold appetizer or main
course for a summer lunch. This
is a pleasant opportunity to
experiment with combinations of
herbs and mushrooms. Use
milky caps, chanterelles,
hedgehog mushrooms, or
common store mushrooms.

½ pound mushrooms, chopped
4 tablespoons butter
1 yellow onion, chopped
6 eggs, beaten
½ cup milk or half and half
¼ cup dry sherry
¼ cup bread crumbs
¼ cup freshly grated Parmesan
    cheese
2 teaspoons chopped fresh
    parsley
½ teaspoon dried tarragon
½ teaspoon dried oregano
½ teaspoon salt
½ teaspoon ground pepper

In a sauté pan or skillet, sauté the mushrooms
in the butter for about 3 minutes. Add the
onion and cook over moderate heat until it is
translucent. Cool.

In a mixing bowl, blend the eggs, milk,
sherry, bread crumbs, Parmesan cheese,
herbs, salt, and pepper. Stir in the mushrooms
and onion and spread the mixture in a greased
9-by-13-inch baking pan. Bake for 30 minutes
in a preheated 350° oven or until a knife
inserted in the center comes out clean. Cool,
then cut into squares to serve.

—*Ken Kassenbrock and Pat Bedinger*

Mushroom Omelette

Serves 3 to 4 as a main course

The flavor of mild and delicate mushrooms, such as oyster, puffball and shaggy mane mushrooms, is enhanced when cooked with eggs. Slicing mushrooms finely allows them to cook more quickly.

½ pound mushrooms, thinly
    sliced
4 tablespoons butter
¼ cup chopped fresh chives
¼ cup chopped fresh parsley
¼ cup heavy cream
6 eggs, which have been kept at
    room temperature for at least
    30 minutes and then lightly
    beaten
Salt and pepper to taste

In a sauté pan or skillet, sauté the mushrooms in 2 tablespoons of the butter. Cook until the liquid has almost evaporated. Add the chives and parsley. Set aside.

Blend the cream into the eggs. Melt the remaining 2 tablespoons of butter in an omelette pan. Add the beaten eggs, salt, and pepper. Allow the eggs to partially cook, then add the mushroom mixture. Quickly fold the omelette in half and transfer to warm plates.

—Louise Freedman

Mushroom Soufflé

Serves 2 or 3 as a main course

Try using chanterelles and/or blewits for color as well as gustatory pleasure.

4 tablespoons butter
1 small onion, minced
¾ pound mushrooms, minced
¼ cup flour
1 cup half and half
¼ cup dry sherry
1 tablespoon chopped fresh
    parsley
½ teaspoon salt
½ teaspoon ground white pepper
Dash of cayenne
4 eggs, separated
2 tablespoons bread crumbs

In a sauté pan or skillet, melt the butter and sauté the onion until translucent. Add the mushrooms and cook slowly for about 7 to 10 minutes or until most of the liquid has evaporated. Add the flour; cook and stir for 2 or 3 minutes, then mix in the half and half and sherry. Add the parsley, salt, pepper, and cayenne. Cool.

Beat the egg yolks and add to the cooled mushroom mixture. Beat the egg whites until stiff. Fold them gently into the mushroom-egg yolk mixture, then turn into a buttered 6-cup soufflé dish. Sprinkle the bread crumbs on top. Bake in a preheated 350° oven for about 45 minutes or until the top is firm and golden brown.

—Louise Freedman

Curried Rice with Mushrooms

Serves 4 as a side dish

The use of curry powder demands a mushroom with strong flavor, such as the common store mushroom, shaggy parasol, horse mushroom, or candy cap.

2 cups water
Salt to taste
1 cup brown rice
4 tablespoons butter
¼ cup chopped onion
¼ cup chopped celery
½ pound mushrooms, chopped
¾ tablespoon curry powder
¼ cup chutney, minced
¼ cup pine nuts
2 tablespoons raisins, chopped

In a saucepan, bring the water to a boil, add the salt, and stir in the rice. Reduce the heat to low. Cover and steam 35 to 40 minutes or until tender.

In a sauté pan or skillet, melt the butter and sauté the onion, celery, and mushrooms for about 5 to 6 minutes. Stir in the curry powder and continue to blend until the vegetables are nicely browned. Add the chutney to the curry mixture and fold the entire mixture into the brown rice. Add the pine nuts and raisins just before serving.　　　　*—Roma Wagner*

Mushroom Pilaf

Serves 6 as a side dish

Many mushroom varieties can go into this dish.

2 tablespoons butter
1 medium onion, diced very fine
2 cups long-grain white rice
¼ pound mushrooms, sliced
3½ cups beef broth

Melt the butter in a large sauté pan or skillet. Add the onion and rice, stirring until golden brown in color. Stir in the mushrooms, and then the beef broth. Cover.

Bring to a boil and lower the heat to a simmer. Cook for about 20 minutes or until all the broth is absorbed.　　　*— Ardie Drysdale*

Mushroom Risotto

Serves 4 as a side dish

Bland foods such as rice complement the nuances of mushroom flavors. This dish can be accented with many varieties of mushrooms. We recommend shaggy parasols, boletes, or chanterelles.

3 cups chicken broth
Pinch of saffron
4 tablespoons butter
1 tablespoon olive oil
½ pound mushrooms, sliced
1 cup Arborio rice
Salt and pepper to taste
2 tablespoons chopped fresh
parsley
½ cup freshly grated Parmesan
cheese

Place the chicken broth in a saucepan; add the saffron and bring the broth to a boil. Remove from the heat. In a saucepan, melt the butter with the olive oil and sauté the mushrooms for 5 minutes. Add the rice; cook and stir until golden. Add the heated chicken broth 1 cup at a time, simmering and stirring occasionally until each cup is absorbed and the rice is creamy. Add salt and pepper. Sprinkle with parsley.

Serve immediately on a platter with the cheese sprinkled on top.

—Kitchen Magic with Mushrooms

Baked Kasha and Mushrooms

Serves 4 as a side dish

An Eastern European casserole dish, combining the nuttiness of buckwheat groats with the flavor and texture of mushrooms such as milky caps, common store mushrooms or boletes.

1 cup kasha
5 tablespoons butter
3½ cups boiling water
1 medium onion, chopped
1 pound mushrooms, cut into
large pieces
2 tablespoons chopped fresh dill
Salt to taste
½ cup sour cream or plain
yogurt

Wash and rinse the kasha. In a large saucepan, melt 3 tablespoons of the butter. Add the kasha and stir constantly to keep the grains separated and coated for 3 minutes. Stir in the boiling water. Cover and cook for about 10 minutes.

In a sauté pan or skillet, sauté the onion in the remaining 2 tablespoons of the butter. Add the mushrooms and cook until all the liquid is absorbed. Add the chopped dill.

Blend the mushroom mixture into the kasha and add the salt. Place it in a buttered casserole dish. Bake for 15 to 20 minutes in a preheated 350° oven.

Top each serving with a large spoonful of sour cream.

—*Louise Freedman*

Fettuccine with Artichoke Hearts and Mushrooms

Serves 5 or 6 as a main course

The contrasting flavors of artichokes and mushrooms convert pasta into an exciting vegetarian meal. Small trimmed whole artichokes may be used.

Alternate Mushrooms: chanterelle, common store mushroom, puffballs

12 small fresh artichoke hearts, outer leaves removed
¼ cup wine vinegar
6 garlic cloves, minced
½ pound mushrooms, sliced
¼ cup olive oil
4 green onions, cut into 2-inch slices
2 tablespoons fresh lemon juice
Salt and pepper to taste
1 pound fresh or dried *fettuccine*
4 tablespoons unsalted butter
½ cup heavy cream
½ cup minced fresh Italian parsley
Freshly grated Parmesan cheese

In a medium saucepan, simmer the artichokes in water to cover and the vinegar for 5 to 8 minutes or until they can be pierced with a fork. Drain.

In a sauté pan or skillet, sauté the garlic and mushrooms in the olive oil for 5 minutes. Add the green onions and cook until translucent. Add the lemon juice, salt, and pepper. Add the artichokes. Set aside and keep warm.

Cook the *fettuccine* in a large amount of boiling salted water until *al dente.* Drain. Put the *fettuccine* back into the pot, add the butter, and toss the pasta to coat it. Add the cream and quickly toss. Add the artichokes, mushrooms, and parsley and toss again.

Serve this dish in a large platter accompanied with a bowl of Parmesan cheese.

—*Louise Freedman*

Tagliarini with Mushroom and Eggplant Sauce

Serves 6 to 8 as a main course

A very filling combination of foods.

Alternate Mushrooms:
common store mushroom,
shaggy parasol mushroom

1 medium whole eggplant
1½ pounds mushrooms
¼ cup olive oil
3 garlic cloves, diced
1 cup dry white wine
1 large green or red bell pepper,
    peeled and coarsely chopped
1 teaspoon chopped fresh
    rosemary, or ¼ teaspoon
    dried rosemary
3 cups chopped fresh tomatoes,
    or one 15-ounce can peeled
    tomatoes
12 California pitted ripe olives
Salt to taste
1½ pounds *tagliarini*
Freshly grated Parmesan cheese

With a fork, prick the skin of the eggplant and place it on a baking sheet in a preheated 450° oven for 30 minutes or until the outer surface is crusty and brown. Cool. Scoop out the pulp and discard the skin.

In a sauté pan or skillet, sauté the mushrooms in the olive oil for 5 minutes or until browned. Remove from the pan with a slotted spoon.

In the same pan, sauté the eggplant and garlic in the olive oil left over from the mushrooms. Cook over medium heat, stirring constantly, for a few minutes. Add the wine and cook a few minutes longer. Add the pepper, rosemary, tomatoes, olives, salt, and the mushrooms. Continue to cook over low heat while you prepare the pasta.

Cook the *tagliarini* in boiling salted water until *al dente*. Drain and serve the sauce on top of the pasta. Generously sprinkle with Parmesan cheese and serve immediately.

—*Louise Freedman*

Baked Mushrooms

Serves 4 as a side dish

One of the simplest of the many mushroom-butter-cream combinations. Shaggy manes or chanterelles are especially good baked this way.

1 to 2 pounds mushrooms, cut in
    halves
Salt and pepper to taste
5 to 6 tablespoons butter
About 4 tablespoons heavy
    cream

Spread the mushrooms in a long baking pan. Dust lightly with salt and pepper and dot with butter. Cover and bake in a preheated 350° oven for 25 minutes. Pour the cream into the pan and bring to a boil on top of the stove.
    —Kitchen Magic with Mushrooms

Stewed Mushrooms

Serves 4 as a side dish

Another basic mushroom dish— try shaggy parasol mushrooms or common store mushrooms this way.

1 pound small button
    mushrooms
3 tablespoons butter
1 cup sour cream or plain yogurt

In a sauté pan or skillet, sauté the mushrooms in the butter until brown. Add the sour cream and allow it to "stew" at a slow simmer on top of the stove. If using yogurt, simmer it until just heated through. Serve immediately.
    —Kitchen Magic with Mushrooms

Miso-baked Mushrooms

Serves 4 as a side dish

The tangy flavor of *miso* turns mushrooms into a delicious side dish. Serve over rice or grill them until brown and juicy.

Alternate Mushrooms:
common store mushroom, oyster mushroom, shaggy parasol mushroom, *shiitake*

1 tablespoon white or red *miso*
2 minced garlic cloves
½ cup water
½ teaspoon sugar
1 teaspoon Asian sesame oil
   (available in Asian markets)
1 tablespoon sesame seeds
1 pound mushrooms

In a large glass or ceramic bowl, mix and crush the *miso* and garlic in the water with the back of a spoon until blended. Add the sugar, sesame oil, and seeds. Add the mushrooms, cover, and marinate in the refrigerator for 20 minutes or more.

Bake in a preheated 400° oven for 20 minutes or grill for 10 minutes.

—*Louise Freedman*

Goat Cheese and Mushrooms

Serves 4 as a side dish

Lovers of goat cheese will enjoy the combinations in this baked dish.

Alternate Mushrooms:
common store mushroom, shaggy parasol

2 tomatoes, peeled, seeded, and
   thinly sliced
1 pound mushrooms, thinly
   sliced
Salt and pepper to taste
1 teaspoon minced fresh
   tarragon, or ¼ teaspoon dried
   tarragon
½ cup bread crumbs
2 tablespoons butter
2 ounces goat cheese

Cover the bottom of a buttered 8-by-8-inch baking pan with the tomatoes. Layer the mushrooms on top. Add the salt, pepper, and tarragon. In a small sauté pan or skillet, slowly brown the bread crumbs in the butter and then add this mixture to the mushrooms. Crumble the cheese on top and bake in a preheated 400° oven for 20 minutes.   —*Louise Freedman*

Creamed Mushrooms Ukrainian Style

Serves 3 to 4 as a side dish

Chanterelles or blewits are highly recommended here. Serve alongside veal cutlets or veal sausages.

3 tablespoons butter
1 medium onion, chopped
1 pound mushrooms, sliced
2 to 3 teaspoons flour
Salt and pepper to taste
2 to 3 tablespoons sour cream

In a saucepan, melt the butter and add the onion and mushrooms. Cover and cook 20 minutes over low heat. Remove the cover and sprinkle the flour over the mushrooms. Blend. Cook and stir for 1 to 2 minutes. Add the salt, pepper, and sour cream. Heat thoroughly, but do not boil. *—Luba Burrows*

 ## Mushroom Strudel

Serves 4 as a main course

Sheets of flaky *filo* embrace the mushroom filling, making an elegant main course. Any mushroom except Asian varieties may be used.

½ cup (1 stick) butter
1 medium onion, chopped
1 pound mushrooms, chopped
¼ cup dry sherry
2 tablespoons chopped fresh dill, or 1½ teaspoons dried dill
Salt to taste
Freshly ground black pepper to taste
¼ cup sour cream
10 *filo* leaves
½ cup bread crumbs

In a saucepan, melt 3 tablespoons of the butter. Sauté the onion until translucent. Add the mushrooms and cook for 5 minutes, or until all the liquid has evaporated. Add the sherry, dill, salt, and pepper. Allow the mixture to cool. Stir in the sour cream.

Melt the remaining butter in a saucepan. Brush a sheet of the *filo* with melted butter and fit it into an 8-inch baking dish. Repeat 5 times, then sprinkle the bread crumbs over the fifth sheet and add the mushroom mixture. Fold the bottom sheets over the mushroom mixture. Add the other 5 sheets in the same manner, only folding the top sheets down to fit within the baking pan. Brush the top surface with the remaining butter. Score lightly into the portions desired. Bake in a preheated 350° oven for 30 minutes or until golden brown. The strudel will expand in size and become light and flaky. *—Louise Freedman*

Mushroom Bread Pudding

Serves 8 to 10 as a side dish

Several different mushrooms can be featured in this savory pudding, such as chanterelles, common store mushrooms, field mushrooms, candy cap mushrooms, and boletes, fresh or dried. Serve it with rack of lamb or a beef rib roast.

One 1-pound loaf day-old
    French bread, cut into small
    cubes
2½ cups milk or more
2 teaspoons chopped fresh
    Italian parsley
½ teaspoon ground coriander
2 green onions, chopped
2 eggs, slightly beaten
2 small zucchinis
1 pound fresh or 3 ounces dried
    mushrooms, sliced (if using
    dried mushrooms, soak them
    in hot water for about 15
    minutes, squeeze dry, and
    reserve the liquid)
4 tablespoons butter
1 teaspoon salt
1½ teaspoons baking powder
1 cup unbleached all-purpose
    flour

Place the bread cubes in a large mixing bowl. Pour 2 cups of the milk over the bread cubes and let stand for 20 minutes. With your fingers occasionally blend the milk into the bread cubes, breaking the hard bread crusts. Mix the parsley, coriander, green onions, and eggs into the mixture.

Grate the zucchinis, then place them in a clean dish towel and twist it to remove as much liquid as possible. Add it to the bread mixture.

In a sauté pan or skillet, sauté the mushrooms in the butter for 7 minutes. Cool for 5 minutes. Add the mushrooms and remaining ½ cup of milk to the mixture.

Mix the salt, baking powder, and flour together and add it slowly, working it into the bread mixture. Do not overwork the dough. The dough should be lumpy and sticky. Add more milk if needed.

Place the mixture in a buttered baking dish and bake in a preheated 350° oven for 45 minutes to 1 hour, or until well browned.

—Louise Freedman

Mushroom Pirog

Serves 4 to 6 as a main course

A mushroom pie, brown and crusty. Blewits are perfect for this dish, but other types of mushrooms are also good.

Filling
2 pounds mushrooms
3 tablespoons butter
6 green onions, chopped
1 teaspoon fresh lemon juice
Salt and pepper to taste
2 tablespoons flour
½ cup milk or more
½ cup sour cream

Pie Crust
½ cup (1 stick) butter
2 cups unbleached all-purpose
   flour mixed with 1 teaspoon
   salt
½ cup cold water or more

2 hard-cooked eggs, sliced
1 egg yolk, mixed with 1
   teaspoon water
Sesame seeds (optional)

Stem and slice the mushrooms. Save the stems for *duxelles* (see page 16). In a sauté pan or skillet, melt the butter and sauté the mushrooms for 5 minutes. Add the green onions, lemon juice, and salt and pepper to taste. Sprinkle the flour on top and, quickly stirring, add milk to blend. Allow it to cool. Add the sour cream. Set aside.

To make the crust, cut the butter into the flour with a pastry cutter or 2 knives. Mix in the water until it forms a ball. You may need additional water. Divide the dough in half. Roll out one dough ball on a floured board and line the bottom of the pie pan.

Fill with the mushroom mixture, then cover the filling with the sliced hard-cooked eggs. Roll out the other half of the crust and cover, pinching the edges securely together. Cut a slit in the top. You may want to form a mushroom design out of the leftover crust to put on top. Brush the top with the egg-water. Sprinkle with sesame seeds, if you like.

Bake in a preheated 350° oven for 30 minutes or until the crust is golden brown.

—Kitchen Magic with Mushrooms

Mushroom Piroshki Variation

Makes 6 turnovers

Use the same ingredients as in the preceding recipe to make beautiful individual turnovers.

Follow the recipe for the *pirog* crust, preceding. Roll the pastry ⅛ inch thick and cut into six 4-inch-diameter circles.

Prepare the mushroom filling. Chop the hard-cooked eggs. Place 1½ tablespoons of cooled filling on half of each circle. Sprinkle some chopped hard-cooked egg on top. Moisten the edge of the circle and fold over, pinching the edges together. Transfer the piroshki to a buttered baking sheet. Brush the egg-water mixture on top. Sprinkle on sesame seeds, if you like. Bake in a preheated 400° oven for about 15 minutes, or until the crusts are golden.

—Kitchen Magic with Mushrooms

PART THREE

A Cook's Encyclopedia of Wild and Cultivated Mushrooms

THE FOLLOWING section describes each mushroom group individually and offers recipes that highlight the group's unique qualities. Most of these mushrooms were selected because they are commercially available, safe to eat, and preferred by mushroom lovers all over the world.

Cooking information has been arranged under separate headings describing how best to clean, cook, and preserve the mushrooms. Additional interesting facts about these life forms are presented so that readers can learn more about the fascinating world of fungi.

Black Saddle Mushroom
(Helvella lacunosa)

THESE BLACK, wrinkle-capped mushrooms occur late in the winter on the West Coast. They have thick, convoluted, and sometimes shiny or slick rounded caps. The broad, hollow, pale-gray stems are fluted and scooped out. Millipedes and insects frequently use these crevices as temporary homes. They can easily be evicted while cleaning.

H. lacunosa is frequently found in large numbers in California, especially under Monterey pines and oak trees. These mushrooms are found scattered in hardwood or conifer forests, but seldom in as large numbers as around cultivated and landscaped places. In the eastern United States they show up in smaller numbers. They appear in many stages of development, from small erupting fruits to crumbling, decomposing older individuals. The small ones are the most favored.

Black saddle mushrooms have deep-black caps and firm, dry, rubbery, whitish stems. In general, there are few look-alikes for this species. But beware of a common white to pink mold that attacks and coats the surface of the cap. It can cause stomach upsets.

Cleaning

Remove any leaves, insects, or pine needles and debris, using a little water. Trim the stem.

Cooking

The flavor of *H. lacunosa* is subtle, and the interesting rubbery stem will give your dishes an unusual texture. Sometimes a dark pigment is released in cooking.

Most mushroom field guides caution users of *H. lacunosa* to either dry or parboil this mushroom for 3 to 5 minutes before cooking because it may contain a small amount of a toxic substance. This material, mono-methylhydrazine, escapes into the air when the mushroom is dried, and it is cooked out when parboiled in water. The water should be discarded.

These mushrooms may be cross-sectioned and cooked in cheese sauce, or deep-fried until crisp. They can be simply sautéed with onions, or cooked in an omelette with chopped parsley. They also go well with rice.

Dried *H. lacunosa* absorbs water easily, so no soaking is needed prior to cooking.

Preserving

These mushrooms may be either dried or pickled. They should be parboiled before pickling. Discard the boiled water.

Black-eyed Pasta

Serves 4 as a main course

The black saddle mushroom stands out dramatically against white pasta. The texture of the mushroom complements asparagus.

Alternate Mushrooms:
black chanterelle, morels

1 to 1½ pounds fresh or 2 to 3
   ounces dried black saddle
   mushrooms
4 tablespoons butter
1½ tablespoons olive oil
6 green onions, sliced
2 cups chopped ham
½ pound asparagus, sliced into
   small pieces
½ cup rich chicken broth
1 pound *fettuccine* or *tagliarini*
½ cup half and half
Freshly grated Parmesan cheese

If using fresh black saddle mushrooms, drop the mushrooms into boiling water to cover. Lower the heat and simmer for 3 to 5 minutes; the mushrooms should remain slightly *al dente;* drain and discard the water. There is no need to soak dried black saddle mushrooms.

Heat the butter and oil in a large saucepan and sauté the onions until translucent. Add the ham and sauté briefly. Then add the asparagus and broth. Simmer for about 5 minutes.

Cook the pasta in a large amount of boiling salted water until *al dente;* drain. Add the ham and asparagus mixture to the pasta along with the mushrooms and half and half. Cook over low heat until heated through.

Serve with grated Parmesan cheese.

— *Camilla Barry*

Beef Stew with Black Saddle Mushrooms

Serves 4 as a main dish

A blend of beef and black saddle mushrooms, to be served over rice and accompanied with a rich cabernet sauvignon or burgundy for a robust meal.

Alternate Mushrooms:
common store mushroom,
shaggy parasol mushroom

1 pound fresh or 3 ounces dried
   black saddle mushrooms,
   coarsely chopped
1½ pounds chuck steak, cut into
   ½-inch strips
½ cup flour
¼ cup mild vegetable oil
1 large onion, sliced
1 or 2 green bell peppers, sliced
2 cups chicken broth
3 tablespoons soy sauce
1 to 2 tablespoons tomato paste
1¼ pounds Italian tomatoes,
   coarsely chopped
Salt

If using fresh black saddle mushrooms, drop the mushrooms into boiling water to cover. Lower the heat and simmer for 3 to 5 minutes; the mushrooms should remain slightly *al dente;* drain and discard the water. There is no need to soak dried black saddle mushrooms.

Dredge the meat in the flour. Heat 3 tablespoons of the oil in a 3- to 4-quart Dutch oven and cook the meat until browned. Remove with a slotted spoon and set aside. Add the remaining 1 tablespoon oil and cook the onions and green peppers over medium heat for about 5 minutes. Mix the broth, soy sauce, and tomato paste together, and add to the pot along with the mushrooms, meat, and tomatoes. Cover the pot and bake in a preheated 325° oven for about 1 to 1½ hours or until the meat is tender. Add salt as necessary. —*Monique Carment*

Day and Night Rice

Serves 4 as a side dish

The subtle flavor of the black saddle mushroom and the contrasting color of the rice makes this an unusual side dish. Serve with any meat or fish, and a tossed salad.

Alternate Mushrooms:
black chanterelle, *shiitake*

6 to 8 fresh or 4 to 5 dried black
   saddle mushrooms
2 cups water
½ teaspoon salt
1 cup long-grain rice
2 tablespoons butter
½ cup slivered blanched
   almonds

If using fresh black saddle mushrooms, drop the mushrooms into boiling water to cover. Lower the heat and simmer for 3 to 5 minutes; the mushrooms should remain slightly *al dente;* drain and discard the water. There is no need to soak dried black saddle mushrooms.

Bring the water and salt to a boil in a heavy medium-sized saucepan. Stir in the rice, reduce to a simmer, cover, and cook for 20 minutes. While the rice is steaming, slice the parboiled mushrooms or break the dried mushrooms in small pieces. In a small sauté pan or skillet, melt the butter and sauté the mushrooms for about 5 minutes. Add the slivered almonds. Stir for another few minutes until the almonds are golden, then set aside. When the rice is done, allow it to rest off the heat for at least 5 minutes. Add the mushrooms and toss to mix.   *—Ed Aguilar*

Blewit
(Clitocybe nuda)

THE WORD *blewit* is an Old English contraction for "blue hat." The blewit is a medium-sized purple blue-capped mushroom with gills and stem of the same color. It drops pale-lilac spores. The cap fades to gray-brown with time. When young, the stem is fleshy and bulblike. The blewit has a clean and unique odor, varying according to where it has grown. Its scientific name has been changed so many times in the past fifteen years that many mushroom hunters have decided to use the old common name of blewit—which hasn't changed in hundreds of years.

This purple-colored mushroom commonly grows in rings in open areas and under a variety of trees, including Monterey cypresses, acacias, oaks, and eucalyptuses. Those found under eucalyptus trees may have a disagreeable odor and taste when cooked. Young firm mushrooms are the most desirable.

The size and shape of *Tricholoma flavovirens* (formerly named *equestre*), a yellow forest mushroom with a sticky cap commonly called "man on horseback," is similar to the blewit, and, after peeling the cap, it is cleaned and cooked by mushroom enthusiasts in the same manner as the blewit. These mushrooms make a very pleasant dish when cooked with chicken broth and onions. Their flavor and texture are retained well after cooking.

Cleaning

Trim bases of any matted material. Brush the caps and stems with a little water, and drain on paper towels. Discard caps clearly invaded by insect larvae, and trim the affected parts. Insects are as fond of blewits as we are.

Cooking

This mushroom sautés beautifully. Sour cream combines with blewits especially well. Young caps are excellent pickled or marinated, after having been cooked.

Blewits have the unique ability of retaining their purple-blue hue after cooking. This offers the chef an opportunity to create a dinner using exciting color contrasts. For instance, a soufflé prepared with blewits sliced lengthwise and thin zucchini rounds produces an appetizing color and taste combination. A lovely purple aspic can be prepared from this attractive mushroom. Blewits are tasty prepared as *duxelles* (see page 16).

Preserving

Sauté in butter and freeze. Dried blewits lose much of their flavor. Blewits can also be pickled whole, if small, or sliced and kept in the refrigerator for that special unannounced guest.

Jellied Blewit Soup

Serves 4 as a first course

A delightful dark-purple jellied soup to serve on a summer day.

1 pound blewits, chopped
4½ to 5 cups chicken broth
2 tablespoons dry sherry
Salt and pepper
1 envelope (1 tablespoon) plain
   gelatin
¼ cup cold water
Crème fraîche or sour cream
Minced fresh chives

In a large saucepan, simmer the mushrooms in 4½ cups of chicken broth for 30 minutes. Strain through cheesecloth in a bowl, pressing the pulp to extract all the liquid. Discard the pulp.

Measure the liquid and add more broth if necessary to make 4 cups. Add the sherry and salt and pepper to taste. Soften the gelatin in the cold water. Allow it to stand for 5 minutes. Return the soup to the saucepan, bring to a boil, and stir in the gelatin. Pour into individual soup cups and chill in the refrigerator until it jells (4 to 5 hours). Top with a spoonful of *crème fraîche* and sprinkle with the chives.

—Kitchen Magic with Mushrooms

Blewits and Peas

Serves 4 as a side dish

Mint adds an aromatic quality to peas and blewits.

Alternate Mushrooms:
common store mushroom,
shaggy parasol mushroom

4 shallots or green onions,
   minced
4 tablespoons butter
1 pound blewits, diced
1 pound fresh peas or thawed
   frozen green peas
½ cup chicken broth
Salt and pepper to taste
4 teaspoons minced fresh mint

In a sauté pan or skillet, sauté the shallots in the butter until translucent. Add the blewits and sauté for 5 minutes. Add the peas and chicken broth, and cook for 6 to 7 minutes. Add the salt, pepper, and mint. Cook for another few minutes or until the peas are tender.   —Kitchen Magic with Mushrooms

Blewits with Tofu

Serves 3 to 4 as a side dish

A blend of tofu, blewits, and ginger that will add color and unusual taste to your meal.

Alternate Mushrooms:
common store mushroom, *shiitake*

1 tablespoon butter
4 blewits, sliced
One ¼-inch slice fresh ginger, peeled and minced
3 to 4 tablespoons soy sauce
1 pound firm tofu, cut into 1-inch cubes

Melt the butter in a sauté pan or skillet. Add the blewits and sauté for 5 to 7 minutes or until the blewits are tender. Add the ginger, soy sauce, and tofu. Simmer and stir for a few minutes. Serve on brown rice.

—*Karel Edith and John Lennie*

Chicken with Blewits and Apple Cider

Serves 4 as a main course

A tangy main course that combines blewits and vegetables with chicken, apple cider, and Calvados.

Alternate Mushroom:
common store mushroom

2 tablespoons butter
1 tablespoon mild vegetable oil
One 2½-pound chicken, cut into serving pieces
Salt and pepper to taste
1 small onion, chopped
12 small blewits
2 tablespoons Calvados
½ cup apple cider
8 small onions
12 baby carrots
1 cup heavy cream
2 egg yolks

Melt the butter with the oil in a large sauté pan or skillet. Sauté the chicken pieces until lightly golden. Season with salt and pepper and add the chopped onion and blewits. Sauté about 3 minutes more. Add the Calvados, a rather expensive apple brandy from France, and apple cider, cover tightly, and cook over low heat for about 30 minutes. With a slotted spoon remove the chicken, onion, and mushrooms to a warm platter and keep warm in the oven.

Steam the small onions and carrots separately in a steamer until they are just tender; set aside. Slowly stir the cream into the sauté pan or skillet and bring to a boil. Add the yolks by first stirring some hot cream into them, then stir this mixture into the pan, using a whisk and stirring briskly. Simmer, stirring constantly, for 1 minute.

Arrange the steamed vegetables on top of the mushrooms, onions, and chicken. Pour the sauce over all and serve immediately.

—*Roma M. Wagner*

Fillet of Sole with Blewit Duxelles

Serves 4 as a main course

Here is an opportunity to use *duxelles* in a mildly flavored dish.

Alternate Mushrooms:
black saddle mushroom,
common store mushroom

Sauce
2 tablespoons butter
2 teaspoons minced green onions
2 tablespoons flour
1½ cups milk, warmed
½ cup rich chicken broth
⅛ teaspoon ground white pepper
Dash of Tabasco sauce
Pinch of dried thyme
½ cup *duxelles* (see page 16)
½ cup heavy cream

8 sole fillets
2 tablespoons butter
1 tablespoon safflower oil
¼ cup freshly grated Parmesan
   cheese

In a heavy saucepan, melt the butter and cook the onions until translucent. Mix in the flour and stir until golden. Slowly add the milk, chicken broth, white pepper, Tabasco, and thyme. Whisk until smooth and thick. Add the *duxelles* and stir in well. Slowly add the cream and blend well.

Cut each sole fillet in half. In a sauté pan or skillet, lightly brown the fish on both sides in the butter and oil over medium heat. Place a generous tablespoon of sauce in each dish. Place 2 pieces of the browned sole on the sauce. Top with more sauce and sprinkle with 1 tablespoon of Parmesan cheese.

Place under a preheated broiler until the sauce is bubbling and the top is brown.
                  —Kitchen Magic with Mushrooms

Boletes
(Boletus, Leccinum, Suillus)

IF THERE is a universally popular wild mushroom, it may be *Boletus edulis*. The French refer to them affectionately as *cèpes,* the Germans glorify them as *Steinpilz,* and the Italians are wild about their *porcini,* meaning piglets (pigs compete for them). The Swedish refer to their treasures as *stensopp*. In Poland, *borowik* are canned and sold in the market. The Russians claim *byelii-greeb* sustained them during wartime when other food was not available. In this country, *B. edulis* is sometimes called "king bolete."

Many people use different types of these "hamburger bun," brown-capped, bulbous-stemmed, pore-bearing early fall delicacies interchangeably with *B. edulis.* Most mushroom hunters commonly refer to all of these mushrooms as "boletes." In this book, we will refer to fresh *B. edulis* as *cèpes,* and dried *B. edulis* as *porcini.* The genus *Leccinum,* "scaber stalk mushrooms," with white pores and black scales on their white pillarlike stems, and the genus *Suillus,* "slippery jacks," with sticky caps, gray-white to yellow pores, and narrower stems, are among the edible boletes. However, those with red pores must be avoided. They are dangerous.

In general, fresh firm specimens are best for cooking or drying. Discard wormy ones or those with soft brown decomposing flesh.

Leccinum and *Suillus* as a rule grow in association with specific trees in a variety of plant communities. By contrast, *B. edulis* is most commonly found in pine forests.

Boletes are different from other mushrooms in that they have pores rather than gills on the underside of the cap. Spores are released by the thousands from the inner walls of hundreds of tiny round tubes making up the lower cap surface. This spore-bearing area resembles and acts like a sponge.

About ten days after the first heavy rains fall in the west, in September or October, young forms begin mounding up the pine needles under the trees. In the east, this occurs during the summer months. They are frequently found in large numbers. Specimens of differing ages are found at the same time. In some locations the season can last for four or five weeks. *B. edulis* is indeed grand and hardy to behold, with its fat, bulbous stem decorated at the top with a network of lacy white veins and its nourishing brown cap held high above the forest floor.

Leccinum species as a rule are found near madrone, aspen, and birch trees and manzanita bushes.

People from Slavic countries revel when they find species of *Suillus*. These are most often found near pine trees and must be collected young. *Suillus granulatus* has a perfumed odor and is commonly found near Monterey pines. Usually it is pickled for later use.

Older boletes should have their pores removed *at once* if they are soggy or green. This portion of the cap is not good-tasting, cooks poorly, and is impossible to dry. This is not a problem with young firm specimens.

Cleaning Fresh Boletes

The minimum use of water is important. Try not to allow water to enter the pore surface, for it tends to absorb a great deal of moisture. Remove any dark parts of the mushroom. Brush off the caps of *Boletus* and *Leccinum*. Peel off slimy tops of *Suillus*. If old, gently separate the spongy material from below the cap, using your finger or a knife, and peel off carefully. Check the underside of the cap for worm holes. If there are many, discard the cap. If only a few exist, use the parts not affected.

Cooking Fresh Boletes

These mushrooms can be slippery. To reduce this quality, quickly fry slices in oil or butter. The simplest method of preparation is to sauté them in olive oil and butter, then add a rich brown sauce and serve as a side dish with steak, broiled chicken, or fish. Or layer fried mushrooms over rice, or baked or mashed potatoes. Another way to quickly prepare boletes is to dip thick slices in beaten eggs, then dust in seasoned bread crumbs for deep-frying.

It has been observed that the fresh *Boletus edulis* flown here from Italy has a stronger odor and taste than the same mushroom found in this country. From this and from similar observations made of other mushrooms, it may be concluded that botanically identical species of mushrooms from different localities may have noticeably dissimilar characteristics of size, odor, and taste. This suggests that, in part, subtle chemical and physical differences may result from the habitat in which the mushrooms grow.

Preserving

Boletes change rapidly. They should be used or preserved as soon as you bring them home.

In the United States, the most common method of preserving boletes is to dry them. Cut them into lengthwise slices no less than ½ inch thick from cap to base including the stems (see Drying Mushrooms, page 11).

Boletes may be frozen and stored uncooked after being sliced into ¼-inch slices and placed in a freezer bag. They will keep well for 6 months (see Freezing Mushrooms, page 12).

Pickled boletes may serve as a conversation piece for your cocktail party.

Cooking with Dried Boletes

As a rule, 3 ounces of dried boletes will equal 1 pound of rehydrated mushrooms. Much variation is found in chefs' opinions as to how long to soak them. On the average they are soaked for about 15 minutes in warm water to cover. Heat hastens the rehydration process. The length of time depends upon the thickness of the slices. Squeeze dry, but be sure to save the liquid in the bowl to preserve the rich flavor for use in your dish.

Dried boletes have a deep, rich taste that dominates soups and sauces for polentas and pastas. When you cook with dried *B. edulis* your kitchen will be redolent with its powerful fragrance. The essence of the mushroom persists in the cooking pot even after the pot has been washed and dried.

Cut mushrooms into desired sizes after soaking. In general, the larger the pieces, the more flavor. Some chefs prefer to sauté them quickly in olive oil and butter before adding them to the dish they are preparing. Add the remaining soaking liquid to your food preparation by carefully pouring off the concentrated essence from the top, discarding any residual matter such as sand or soil at the bottom of the vessel.

Commercially Dried Boletes

Dried bulk or bagged boletes command high prices in the marketplace. The imported Italian boletes (*porcini*) are usually dark in appearance, and their smell is intense and aromatic. Home-dried preparations do not have the same odor and are lighter in color. Old-timers claim that dried mushrooms develop a deeper, more robust aroma if kept for two or three years.

When you shop for dried boletes, inspect them carefully to be certain there are no gilled caps present. Sometimes mushrooms of lesser quality are mixed with or substituted for *B. edulis*. Bagged products may also contain broken and granulated brittle pieces of fungi which will not reconstitute well and have little taste. Purchase only solid, clean, thickly sliced mushrooms.

Imported Polish boletes seem to require long soaking periods. They must be reconstituted overnight before cooking.

Brown Sauce with Boletes

Makes about 2½ cups

A hearty brown sauce to serve with grilled steaks.

Alternate Mushroom:
shaggy parasol mushroom

4 cups rich beef, veal, or poultry broth
3 cups full-bodied zinfandel wine
2 tablespoons minced shallots or green onions
4 tablespoons butter
½ to 1 pound boletes, chopped

In a heavy saucepan, reduce the broth and wine over high heat until it starts to thicken, then lower the heat and reduce to 1½ or 2 cups. Remove from the heat. Sauté the shallots in the butter in a saucepan. Raise the heat. Add the mushrooms and sauté until most of the juice evaporates. Add the reduced broth and wine mixture.

To use this sauce with steak, deglaze the pan with red wine or brandy and add to the sauce.

—*Paul Johnston*

Creamed Potatoes and Mushrooms

Serves 4 as a side dish

Fresh boletes are cut into the same size as new potatoes and baked in a Madeira-cream sauce.

Alternate Mushrooms:
common store mushroom, hedgehog mushroom

1½ to 2 pounds new potatoes
2 to 3 firm young boletes
3 to 4 tablespoons butter
2 tablespoons flour
½ cup half and half
½ cup Madeira
Salt and pepper to taste

Cook the potatoes in boiling salted water to cover until tender. Drain; peel the skins and cut into cubes. Set aside.

Cut the mushrooms into cubes similar in size to the potatoes. In a saucepan, sauté the mushrooms in the butter. Remove them with a slotted spoon when they are browned. Mix the flour into the juices remaining in the saucepan. Add half and half and whisk over low heat until thickened. Add the Madeira and allow the sauce to thicken again. Add salt and pepper to taste.

In a buttered casserole dish, mix the potatoes and mushrooms together. Pour the sauce on top and bake in a preheated 350° oven for 20 minutes or until it is brown and bubbly.

—*Louise Freedman*

Italian Mushroom Gravy

Makes about 5 cups

The strong flavor of dried Italian boletes makes an outstanding gravy. Serve over ravioli, pasta, polenta, or use for a chicken *cacciatore*. Sprinkle freshly grated Romano cheese on top.

Alternate Mushrooms:
common store mushroom, shaggy parasol mushroom

3 ounces dried Italian boletes
  (*porcini*)
1 pound lean ground beef
2 Italian sausages, cut into
  pieces
1 large onion, chopped
2 garlic cloves, minced
¼ cup chopped fresh parsley
Chopped fresh or dried
  rosemary, sage, oregano, or
  basil to taste
One 6-ounce can tomato paste
1 cup dry white wine
Two 8-ounce cans tomato sauce

Soak the mushrooms in warm water to cover for about 15 minutes, squeeze dry and finely mince them. Reserve the liquid. In a large, heavy saucepan, sauté the beef and sausages until lightly browned. Add the onion, garlic, parsley, mushrooms, and herbs. Mix the tomato paste with the wine. Add to the gravy along with the tomato sauce and the soaking liquid from the mushrooms. Simmer until thick, about 30 to 45 minutes.

—Kitchen Magic with Mushrooms

Deep-fried Cèpes

Serves 5 as an appetizer

Make this crunchy treat when *Boletus edulis* is in season.

5 to 8 large *cèpe* (*Boletus*) stems
Oil for deep-frying
Salt to taste

Preheat a deep-fryer to 300° to 330°. Using a vegetable slicer, slice the stems as thin as possible. Spread the slices on paper towels.

Heat the oil very slowly to 380°. Drop a few chips at a time into the fryer basket and cook quickly. Shake the basket or stir so that they don't stick together. Cook until golden in color.

Drain on paper towels and sprinkle with salt.

—*Louise Freedman*

Bavarian Mushroom Soup with Dumplings

Serves 4 as a first course

A variation of a favorite dish served in Germany and Austria, where it is called *Steinpilz auf rheum.*

Alternate Mushrooms:
chanterelle, common store mushroom

2 to 3 small boletes
3 or 4 shallots or green onions, chopped
3 tablespoons butter
2 ounces smoked ham, minced
Pinch of dried rosemary
2 teaspoons chopped fresh parsley
3 tablespoons flour
2 quarts beef or chicken broth
Salt to taste

Dumplings
3 tablespoons minced onion
4 tablespoons butter
3 cups stale French bread, cut into ½-inch cubes
½ to 1 cup milk or half and half
2 tablespoons chopped fresh parsley
⅛ teaspoon ground nutmeg
2 eggs, beaten slightly
Salt to taste
About ½ cup plus 2 tablespoons flour

Cut the caps and stems of the mushrooms into small slices. In a sauté pan or skillet, sauté the shallots in the butter until translucent. Add the mushrooms, ham, rosemary, and parsley. Sprinkle in the flour and stir in the broth. Adjust the taste by adding salt. Simmer for about 15 minutes.

To make the dumplings, in a saucepan sauté the onion in butter until translucent. Add the bread cubes, mixing them with the onions and butter. Remove the bread mixture to a mixing bowl and add the milk, parsley, and nutmeg. Let it stand about 10 minutes. Be careful not to get the bread too wet. Add the eggs and salt and knead with your hands. Add the flour gradually until the mixture holds together and forms a ball.

Moisten your hands with water and form the mixture into round balls. Gently place the dumplings in a large amount of boiling salted, water. Cook them gently over medium heat, occasionally turning them with a slotted spoon for about 10 minutes, or until the balls float to the surface.

Drain the dumplings. Divide them among the soup bowls and pour the hot mushroom soup over them.

—Kitchen Magic with Mushrooms

Stuffed Baked Boletes

Serves 4 to 5 as a side dish

Some bolete caps are large enough to be served cut into quarters or sliced into wedges like pieces of a pie. Shellfish, meat, and spinach can be used for fillings.

Alternate Mushrooms:
common store mushroom, horse mushroom, the prince

3 to 4 boletes
4 tablespoons olive oil or more
2 garlic cloves, minced
2 prosciutto slices, minced
1 egg, slightly beaten
2 tablespoons freshly grated
    Parmesan cheese
½ cup bread crumbs
1 teaspoon minced fresh basil, or
    ¼ teaspoon dried basil
Salt and pepper to taste

Remove the bolete stems and save for another dish or dry the stems for future use. In a sauté pan or skillet, sauté the tops of the mushroom caps in the olive oil for a few minutes or until they turn brown. With a slotted spoon remove them to a warm baking dish. In the oil that remains in the pan, sauté the garlic and prosciutto until the garlic is translucent. Allow the mixture to cool somewhat, then stir in the egg, Parmesan cheese, bread crumbs, basil, salt, and pepper.

Stuff the caps and bake them in a preheated 400° oven for 15 to 20 minutes or until lightly browned. —*Louise Freedman*

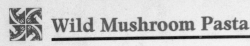

Wild Mushroom Pasta

Makes about 1¼ pounds

A clever way of presenting this delicious mushroom. Serve it with a mushroom cream sauce and/or grate bits of truffle on top.

1 ounce dried Italian boletes (*porcini*)
3 cups unbleached all-purpose flour or more
2 large eggs
Pinch of salt

Soak the mushrooms for about 15 minutes in warm water to cover, squeeze dry, and purée. Reserve the soaking water.

Place the flour in a mound on a pastry board. Make a well in the center of the mound of flour. Crack the eggs into the cavity and add the salt. Add the dried mushrooms.

With a fork, mix the eggs, salt, and mushroom purée. Then slowly start to incorporate the flour from the lower part, pushing it under the dough to keep the compacted dough ball intact and separated from the surrounding loose flour. If the flour fails to hold together during kneading, sprinkle some of the mushroom liquid on it. If the dough is too soft, add more flour. After half the flour has been incorporated into the dough ball, start kneading the mass with the palms of your hands.

Lay the dough ball on top of the flour and continue kneading until the ball has absorbed most of the flour. Sift the leftover flour and set it aside for sprinkling during the rolling and folding steps later.

Cut the dough ball into 2 pieces. Repeat the rolling and folding steps with each of these 2 pieces. Turn the pasta rollers to their widest setting, and feed one of the 2 pieces of dough between the rollers. Remove from the rollers, fold the dough into thirds, and press down. Sprinkle with flour and feed through the rollers again. Repeat the folding, sprinkling, and rolling 8 to 10 times, until the dough is very smooth. Repeat the procedure with the other pieces of dough.

Adjust the roller setting to a narrower notch, and pass the sheet of dough through only once. Do not fold again. Now move the rollers to each successively narrower notch, passing the dough through each notch only once, until the sheet is paper thin.

If you don't have a pasta machine, knead the dough for about 10 minutes, until smooth and elastic, then divide the dough in half and roll each piece to a thickness of ⅛ inch or less.

Lay the completed sheet of dough on a floured surface to dry for 15 minutes before cutting, and proceed with the forming of the second sheet.

To cut *fettuccine,* pass each sheet of pasta through the wide teeth of the cutting section of the pasta machine, or cut by hand into ¼-inch ribbons. —*Mary Etta Moose, Washington Square Bar and Grill*

Mushroom-Zucchini Bread

Makes 1 loaf

This hearty bread is strongly flavored by the boletes. The grated zucchini keeps the bread moist.

1 medium-sized zucchini
3 to 4 tablespoons dried boletes
½ cup (1 stick) butter, melted
2½ cups unbleached all-purpose flour
2 tablespoons sugar
2 teaspoons baking powder
½ teaspoon baking soda
1 teaspoon salt
½ cup freshly grated Romano cheese
2 eggs
1 cup buttermilk

Grate the zucchini, then place it in a clean dish towel and twist it to remove as much liquid as possible. Grind the mushrooms in a blender or food processor, allowing the fine particles to settle before removing the cover. Mix the ground mushrooms into the melted butter and allow it to cool somewhat. In a bowl, combine the flour, sugar, baking powder, baking soda, salt, and ¼ cup of the cheese. In a mixing bowl, beat the eggs slightly. Add the buttermilk and grated zucchini. Mix the dry ingredients into the egg-zucchini mixture (do not overbeat). Add the butter-mushroom mixture and blend.

Spoon into a greased loaf pan and sprinkle the remaining cheese on top. Bake in a preheated 350° oven for 55 to 60 minutes or until it is brown and crusty on top. Cool 10 minutes before removing from pan.

— *Gary Forrest*

A Meal of Boletes, Modena Style

Serves 2 as an appetizer and main course

Two to three *Boletus edulis,* weighing about 3 pounds total, are enough to provide a meal for two people. The caps are sliced and then deep-fried for an appetizer, and the stems are chopped, sautéed with shallots and cream, and made into a sauce to serve over *tagliarini.*

Deep-fried Boletes
2 to 3 young *cèpe* (*Boletus*) caps
Flour
Oil for deep-frying
Salt and pepper to taste
1 lemon, cut into wedges

Remove the stems from the mushrooms and reserve. Cut the mushrooms into ½-inch slices and dip them in flour. Deep-fry at 375° until golden brown. Remove with a slotted spoon and drain on paper towels. Sprinkle with salt and pepper and serve with lemon wedges.

Tagliarini al Porcini
4 to 5 shallots or green onions
2 to 3 young *cèpe* (*Boletus*)
    stems, chopped
5 tablespoons butter
Juice of ½ lemon
1½ cups heavy cream or half
    and half
Salt and pepper to taste
½ pound fresh *tagliarini*
Freshly grated Romano or
    Parmesan cheese

In a sauté pan or skillet, sauté the shallots and chopped stems in butter until hazel colored. Add the lemon juice. Add the cream, salt, and pepper and cook at a very low temperature for about 10 minutes, stirring gently.

Cook the pasta in a large amount of boiling salted water until *al dente,* then drain.

Pour the sauce over the pasta in a serving bowl. Generously sprinkle the cheese on top.
—*Robert Mackler*

Chicken Fricassée with Boletes

Serves 4 as a main course

Serve this dish with wild rice and a white wine.

Alternate Mushroom:
common store mushroom

2 ounces dried boletes
1 garlic clove, minced
1 small onion, chopped
3 tablespoons butter
3 tablespoons olive oil
One 2½- to 3½-pound chicken, cut into quarters
3 fresh tomatoes, chopped, or one 15-ounce can peeled tomatoes
1 teaspoon chopped fresh thyme, or ¼ teaspoon dried thyme
½ cup dry white wine
Salt and pepper to taste

Soak the mushrooms in warm water for about 15 minutes. Squeeze dry and chop into small pieces. Reserve the mushroom liquid.

In a sauté pan or skillet, sauté the mushrooms, garlic, and onion in the butter for about 3 minutes. Remove the mushrooms with a slotted spoon, leaving some of the butter in the pan. Set the mushrooms aside. In the same saucepan, add the oil and sauté the chicken until browned. Add the mushrooms, tomatoes, herbs, wine, and reserved mushroom liquid. Add salt and pepper to taste. Cover and cook over low heat for about 30 to 45 minutes or until the chicken is tender. *—Louis Maraviglia*

Roast Turkey with Porcini

Alternate Mushroom:
truffles

The next time you roast a turkey, insert small pieces of unsoaked dried Italian boletes (*porcini*) under the skin of the breast of the turkey. You may also want to add a small handful of soaked *porcini* to a simple bread stuffing; use the soaking liquid to moisten the stuffing. The strong flavor of the *porcini* will penetrate throughout the meat. *—Loraine Berry*

Chanterelle
(Cantharellus cibarius)

THIS PLEASANTLY aromatic fleshy wild mushroom shines like an exotic golden flower when seen from a distance against the drab autumn forest background. Also known as "golden chanterelle" and "egg mushroom," it has a magical appeal for most culinary experts in Europe, the United States, and Asia. But all chanterelles are not alike. European and Asian forms are usually about the size of a thumb. In the eastern United States they are the size of a fist. But, ah, in the west they can be as large as two hand spans—from little finger to little finger. Chanterelles weighing as much as two pounds are not uncommon.

Europeans and easterners claim that their varieties are tastier than those from the West Coast and suggest that flavor is more important than thumb size. It has been a rewarding experience to try to resolve this argument. The reader may happily experiment with such savory adventures as are suggested in this book to discover the truth.

Chanterelles seem to be worth their weight in gold. They are golden looking, golden tasting, and golden priced. The cap is fleshy, with wavy, rounded cap margins tapering downward to meet the stem. The gills are not the usual thin straight panels hanging from the lower surface of the cap, as we see in the common store mushroom. Instead, the ridges are rounded, blunt, shallow, and widely spaced. At the edge of the cap they are forked and interconnected. The chanterelle's aroma is variously described as apricot- or peachlike. It is unmistakably different and identifiable.

Chanterelles will reappear in the same places year after year if carefully harvested so as not to disturb the ground in which the mycelium (the vegetative part of the mushroom) grows. There are yearly variations—some years more mushrooms, some less. They fruit from September to February on the West Coast and almost all summer in the east, sometimes coming up in several flushes. We think of them as promiscuous in their plant relationships, because we have found their mycelial threads intertwined with the roots of hardwood trees, conifers, shrubs, and bushes. They enjoy deep, old leaf litter. Chanterelles are seldom invaded by insects. And forest animals do not share our interest in them as food.

There is an off-white species of chanterelle, called *C. subalbidus,* the white chanterelle, found in California and the Pacific Northwest. They are found in the same localities as *C. cibarius,* and we clean and cook them in the same manner as the golden ones. In general, they are more difficult to clean because of their fragility. They are seldom found in large numbers.

A black relative of the chanterelle, *Craterellus cornucopioides,* is unfairly called "the trumpet of death." Don't believe it—the black chanterelle is delicious. *C. cornucopioides* is difficult to spell and to find. Smaller in size than the orange chanterelle, the caps are funnel shaped and hollow all the way down to the base of the stem. It has been well described as a black petunia. Its dark cap, gray underside, and its habit of growing in dark places under shrubs make this secretive mushroom a challenge to find. There are a few equally edible look-alikes.

C. cornucopioides can be halved and easily washed off. The texture is crisp and firm, like the Asian wood ear mushroom, but it is much more tasty. Add it to soups or stews for texture and flavor. Sauté it in butter, or chop and simmer in a white sauce, then serve on thin slices of toast. Many people dry these mushrooms thoroughly and grind them into a powder. This is sprinkled on top of foods or added to casseroles or soups for a rich mushroom flavor.

A Word About Purchasing Commercial Chanterelles

More and more golden chanterelles are appearing in marketplaces. They are expensive, so only buy specimens in prime condition. Here is what to look for:

1. They should have a fragrant odor.
2. The color should be golden or apricot.
3. They should not be slimy or have dark, decaying parts.
4. The gills should not be granular, fragmenting off the fleshy portion of the mushrooms.

Cleaning

This can be a chore. Chanterelles grow exuberantly. The cap margins fold tightly to form crevices from which it is difficult to dislodge debris.

The caps grow around twigs and brambles. Sometimes it is necessary to section portions of larger specimens to get at the foreign material. Use a toothbrush or a nylon mushroom brush to whisk away any surface material. In order to clean small particles of sand or dirt caught between the rounded gills, you must brush them under a slowly running faucet. Do not soak them. In general, the less water the better. Drain them on paper towels. They keep well if allowed to remain in a waxed paper or brown paper bag in the refrigerator until they are cleaned. However, cleaned chanterelles may also be stored in the refrigerator for a few days. They should be loosely arranged in a bowl lined with cloth or paper towels and covered lightly with towels.

Cooking

Cut them into hunks of a generous size, so that the maximum amount of flavor can be appreciated. Chanterelles are meaty and chewy. One of the best ways to cook them is to slice and sauté them in butter. Cream or half and half and chicken broth are good additions. Chanterelles bake well and retain their flavor after long cooking. Eggs, chicken, pork, and veal harmonize beautifully with them.

After trying many recipes, we still prefer to cook chanterelles by baking them for 20 minutes in chicken broth with coarsely chopped onions. Serve this over rice or pasta. Potatoes will overpower the chanterelle flavor, as will many other vegetables.

Very few people eat chanterelles raw. They are peppery and upsetting, and they can make some people ill. In any case, their finest flavor can only be appreciated when they are thoroughly cooked.

Preserving

Freeze chanterelles after sautéing with butter and onions. When defrosted, they will retain most of their flavor.

Dried chanterelles lose flavor, and the texture of the slices becomes rubbery. A chef recently suggested that dried chanterelles reconstituted in water overnight retain more flavor if the soaking water is included when they are cooked.

To can chanterelles, cut them in big chunks and steam for 20 minutes. Then place the pieces in pint canning jars and cover them with the liquid from the steaming vessel or boiling water to make up the difference. Add ½ teaspoon salt and ½ teaspoon vinegar. Finally, sterilize them for 40 minutes in a pressure cooker at 10 pounds pressure.

Chanterelles can be pickled with various spices and flavorings in vinegar, oil, soy sauce, etc.. They will keep for a week in the refrigerator.

Marinated Chanterelles

Serves 8 as an appetizer

Paul Johnston is a well-known Berkeley chef. He recommends that these marinated chanterelles be eaten as appetizers or be heated and drained to serve over pasta.

1 cup peanut oil or light olive oil
1 pound chanterelles, cut into
    large slices (make sure they
    are dry—waterlogged
    mushrooms won't work)

Marinade
¼ cup fine wine vinegar,
    balsamic or fruit vinegar
1 garlic clove, sliced thin
1 bay leaf
1 teaspoon Dijon mustard
Pinch of fresh herbs (tarragon,
    savory, oregano, or marjoram)
¼ teaspoon salt

In a sauté pan or skillet, heat the oil until it becomes very hot, then add the chanterelles. Toss them in the pan quickly for 3 to 5 minutes; set aside.

Combine all the marinade ingredients. Add the chanterelles and the oil from the pan. Marinate the mushrooms for at least 4 hours in the refrigerator. They will keep for 2 weeks in the refrigerator.   *—Paul Johnston*

Golden Chanterelle Puffs

Makes about 35 puffs

Chanterelle puffs are a light and elegant party food. Serve them with a white wine such as traminer, riesling, or sauvignon blanc.

Alternate Mushroom:
fairy-ring mushroom

1 cup chicken broth
½ pound chanterelles, minced
½ cup (1 stick) butter
½ teaspoon salt
1 cup unbleached all-purpose
    flour
3 eggs

Heat the chicken broth in a heavy medium saucepan. Add the chanterelles, butter, and salt and allow to come to a boil. Stir in the flour, mixing constantly until the mixture is smooth and almost leaves the sides of the pan. Remove from the heat. Beat one egg at a time into the mixture.

Drop tablespoons of the dough onto a buttered cookie sheet, spacing the spoonfuls about 2 inches apart. Bake in a preheated 450° oven for 15 minutes or until firm and golden. Cool the puffs on a rack.

   —Louise Freedman

Wilted Spinach Salad with Chanterelles

Serves 4 as a first course

For color and taste contrast, golden chanterelles and deep-green spinach are a great combination. Serve on warm plates and garnish with wedges of egg, if you like.

Alternate Mushrooms:
common store mushroom, ear mushrooms

½ pound chanterelles, sliced
2 tablespoons fresh lemon juice
5 bacon slices, chopped
1 pound spinach
5 green onions, diced
5 radishes, sliced
3 tablespoons red wine vinegar
Salt and pepper to taste
1 hard-cooked egg, cut in
    wedges (optional)

Parboil the chanterelles for 3 to 5 minutes. Drain. Marinate the chanterelles in the lemon juice for 15 minutes.

In a large sauté pan or skillet, fry the bacon until crisp. Remove the bacon with a slotted spoon and reserve. Discard all but 2 tablespoons of the bacon fat from the pan.

Clean and wash the spinach in several changes of water. Cut away tough stems. Dry the spinach well and mix with the green onions, radishes, and marinated chanterelles.

Heat the bacon fat in the pan. Add the vinegar and bacon and, while still hot, pour it over the spinach mixture and toss. Season to taste. Serve on warm dishes and garnish with wedges of egg.

—*Louise Freedman*

Mushroom Biscuits

Makes 12 biscuits

This quick biscuit recipe is especially good when fresh chanterelles are in season. Common store mushrooms can be substituted.

1 small onion, minced
4 tablespoons butter
½ pound chanterelles, chopped into small pieces
2 teaspoons baking powder
½ teaspoon baking soda
1½ teaspoons salt
2 cups unbleached all-purpose flour
·1 cup milk

In a sauté pan or skillet sauté the onion in the butter for 2 minutes. Add the mushrooms to the pan and cook for 5 to 7 minutes or until most of the liquid has evaporated. Set aside and let cool.

In a mixing bowl, sift the baking powder, baking soda, and salt with the flour. Make a well in the center of the flour mixture and slowly pour in the milk, blending the mixture into a sticky dough. Quickly mix the mushroom mixture into the dough. Do not overmix.

Drop the dough by tablespoons onto a buttered baking sheet or fill buttered muffin pans two-thirds full. Bake 15 to 20 minutes in a preheated 400° oven, or until the biscuits are golden brown. —*Louise Freedman*

Chanterelles in the Oven

Serves 4 as a side dish

Easily prepared, this can be served as a side dish with baked chicken, a roast, or grilled fish. It can also be used as a sauce for pasta or rice.

Alternate Mushrooms:
hedgehog mushroom, milky caps

1 pound chanterelles, cut in halves or quarters
1 onion, chopped
¼ cup rich chicken broth
½ cup heavy cream
Salt and pepper to taste
2 tablespoons minced fresh parsley

Arrange the chanterelles in a buttered casserole dish. Cover with the chopped onion. Cover the dish and bake in a preheated 350° oven for 20 minutes. Remove the cover, add the broth and cream, and continue to bake without the cover for another 15 minutes. Do not allow the cream to boil. Adjust the flavor by adding salt and pepper. Serve with the parsley sprinkled on top. —*Louise Freedman*

Sautéed Chanterelles, Russian Style

Serves 4 as a side dish

This is a very old method of cooking chanterelles that was passed down to Mary by her Russian mother. Serve this dish with fried fresh oysters, and a simple coleslaw made of finely shredded cabbage and paper-thin sliced onions dressed lightly with salt, olive oil, and vinegar. Most other mushrooms can be used in this recipe, except for Asian varieties.

4 bacon slices, cut in 1½-inch
 pieces
1 pound chanterelles, cut into
 pieces
1 medium onion, diced
Salt and pepper to taste
1 to 2 tablespoons sweet or sour
 cream

Fry the bacon until crisp. Leave the bacon in the pan and remove all but 2 tablespoons of fat. Place the mushrooms in a large saucepan and add water to cover. Bring to a boil, then drain immediately and thoroughly. Add the chanterelles and onion to the bacon and cook about 10 minutes over low heat, stirring often. Add salt and pepper to taste. Add the cream just before serving.   *—Mary Keehner*

Artichokes and Chanterelles

Serves 4 as a side dish

Here's a recipe that brings together two West Coast favorites. Trimmed small whole artichokes may also be used.

Alternate Mushroom:
common store mushroom

1 pound fresh or thawed frozen
    artichoke hearts
½ pound chanterelles, sliced
    thin
3 tablespoons butter
2 tablespoons flour
1½ cups milk
½ cup half and half
Salt
¼ cup freshly grated Monterey
    jack or Emmenthaler cheese
Few drops of lemon juice

Cook the artichokes in boiling salted water to cover until tender.

Arrange the artichoke hearts in a buttered baking dish. Place the chanterelles on top. Melt the butter in a saucepan, stir in the flour, and add the milk and half and half. Whisk until the mixture starts to thicken. Reduce the heat and add the salt to taste.

Spoon the sauce over the artichokes and chanterelles, sprinkle with the cheese, and bake in a preheated 350° oven for 15 minutes. Quickly squeeze a few drops of lemon juice on top and serve. —*Fred Cherry*

Chanterelles with Chestnuts and Wine

Serves 4 as a side dish

An elegant side dish to serve during the Christmas holidays when chanterelles and chestnuts are fresh on the West Coast. Serve with a prime rib roast.

Alternate Mushrooms:
common store mushroom,
hedgehog mushroom

3 tablespoons butter
1 pound chanterelles, sliced
18 fresh chestnuts, boiled or
    roasted, peeled, shelled and
    sliced
¼ cup dry sherry
Dash of Tabasco sauce
Salt and pepper to taste

Melt the butter in a large saucepan and cook the mushrooms for 10 minutes or until most of the liquid is released from them. Add the chestnuts and cook for 3 minutes. Add the dry sherry and Tabasco sauce, and season with salt and pepper. —*Esther Whited*

Chicken Breasts with Chanterelles

Serves 4 as a main course

Chanterelles and chicken are a natural combination. Here chicken breasts are poached and cut into small portions. The chanterelles are sautéed and served over the chicken.

Alternate Mushrooms:
shaggy mane, morels

2 cups dry white wine
1 garlic clove, crushed
1 bay leaf
1 parsley sprig
4 single chicken breasts, skinned and boned
1½ pounds chanterelles, chopped
4 tablespoons butter
3 shallots or 1 medium onion, minced
⅓ cup pine nuts
Chopped fresh parsley
Salt and pepper to taste

In a large saucepan, bring the wine, garlic, bay leaf, and parsley to a simmer. Add the chicken, cover, and cook until tender, about 15 minutes. When cool enough to handle, remove the chicken and chop it into small portions. Strain the liquid into a medium saucepan.

In a sauté pan or skillet, sauté the chanterelles in the butter until tender; set aside. Pour the liquid from the mushrooms into the reserved poaching liquid and cook until it becomes slightly thickened.

Add the shallots, pine nuts, chicken, and the chanterelles to the liquid and cook without a cover for 10 minutes. Complete the dish with the parsley, salt, and pepper.   —*Jackie Baydo*

Chicken Baked with Cream and Chanterelles

Serves 4 as a main course

Present this dish with fresh vegetables such as green beans or broccoli, rice, and a fine white wine such as chardonnay.

Alternate Mushrooms:
hedgehog mushroom, milky caps

2 tablespoons butter
1 pound chanterelles, sliced
2 tablespoons fresh lemon juice
2 tablespoons chopped shallots
    or green onions
¼ cup dry vermouth
½ cup heavy cream
One 2½-pound chicken, cut into
    serving pieces and skinned
Salt and pepper to taste
Chopped fresh parsley

Melt the butter in a sauté pan or skillet and add the chanterelles, lemon juice, shallots, and vermouth. Cook over low heat for 20 minutes. Add the cream and cook 5 minutes more.

Season the chicken lightly with salt and pepper. Place the chicken in a shallow ovenproof dish. Pour the sauce over the chicken and cook for 30 to 45 minutes in a preheated 350° oven. Baste occasionally with the pan juices. Adjust the seasoning. Add parsley and serve.   *—Robert Mackler*

Veal with Chanterelles

Serves 4 as a main course

Veal is a superb accompaniment for the delicate flavor of chanterelles.

Alternate Mushrooms:
hedgehog mushroom, oyster mushroom, morels

8 veal scallops
4 tablespoons butter
3 tablespoons minced green
    onions
½ cup dry white wine
⅔ cup beef broth
1 tablespoon cornstarch
¼ cup water
1½ cups half and half
½ pound chanterelles, sliced

Gently pound the veal scallops. In a sauté pan or skillet, melt 2 tablespoons of the butter and sauté the scallops until both sides are brown.

Transfer the scallops to an ovenproof dish and place in a 200° oven to keep warm. Add the onions to the pan and sauté for about 1 minute. Pour in the wine and beef broth, and boil for about 5 minutes. Mix the cornstarch and water in a cup. Add to the wine mixture along with the half and half. Cook until the mixture is slightly thickened.

In the meantime, sauté the chanterelles in the remaining 2 tablespoons of the butter in a small skillet. This should take 3 to 5 minutes. Add the mushrooms and veal to the sauce mixture in the sauté pan and heat thoroughly. Serve with rice.   *—Candice Mick*

Chicken with Chanterelles and Marsala

Serves 4 as a main course

Alternate Mushrooms:
common store mushroom,
hedgehog mushroom, milky caps

4 single chicken breasts, skinned
    and boned
6 tablespoons peanut oil
2 tablespoons soy sauce
1 tablespoon Asian sesame oil
    (available in Asian markets)
1 teaspoon *mirin* or dry sherry
2 garlic cloves, minced
½ to ¾ pound chanterelles,
    sliced
½ teaspoon paprika
2 tablespoons flour
1 cup chicken broth
½ cup dry Marsala wine
Freshly ground black pepper

Marinate the chicken breasts in 2 tablespoons of the peanut oil, soy sauce, sesame oil, *mirin,* and garlic for 2 hours.

In a sauté pan or skillet, cook the mushrooms in 2 tablespoons of the oil slowly to cook off their liquid; set aside. Mix the paprika into the flour. Drain the chicken and roll it in the flour mixture. In another sauté pan or skillet, sauté the chicken in the remaining oil, browning on both sides for 3 minutes. Add the chicken broth, Marsala wine, and the mushrooms. Cover and cook over low heat for 20 minutes or until the chicken is tender. Add pepper to taste.   —*Pat George*

Veal Chops with Chanterelles

Serves 4 as a main course

The Italian name for this dish is *baffi del capitano ai funghi,* "captain's moustache with wild mushrooms," because the curved bones of the veal chops are thought to resemble moustaches.

Alternate Mushroom:
hedgehog mushroom

½ cup water
2 tablespoons butter
1 lemon
1 pound chopped chanterelles
4 loin veal chops with curved
    bones trimmed of fat
1 tablespoon butter or more if
    needed
1 tablespoon olive oil or more if
    needed
4 minced shallots or green
    onions
Salt and pepper to taste
¼ cup heavy cream
Minced fresh parsley

Place the water, butter, and the juice of ½ lemon in a large saucepan. When the water begins to boil, immediately add the chanterelles and simmer 5 minutes. Remove the chanterelles with a slotted spoon. Reduce the cooking liquid until the mushroom flavor is intense.

Sprinkle the chops with juice from the remaining lemon half. Melt the butter with the olive oil in a sauté pan or skillet. Sauté the chops until golden brown on both sides. Remove the chops to a warm platter.

Put the chanterelles in the sauté pan. Add the shallots and the reduced cooking liquid, salt, and pepper. Toss and cook a few minutes. Add the cream and cook down until thickened. Then add the parsley, toss, and serve the sauce over the chops.—*Mary Etta Moose, Washington Square Bar and Grill*

Pork Loin Chops with White Wine

Serves 4 as a main course

Pork loin chops, chanterelles, and a spicy wine such as a gewürztraminer make this an outstanding dish.

Alternate Mushrooms:
common store mushroom, hedgehog mushroom

Four ½-inch-thick pork loin
  chops
2 tablespoons olive oil
2 or more garlic cloves, minced
2 tablespoons butter or more
½ to 1 pound chanterelles,
  chopped
3 tablespoons chopped fresh
  parsley
½ cup dry white wine
Salt and pepper to taste

In a sauté pan or skillet, brown the pork chops in the olive oil. Add the garlic the last few minutes. Remove the garlic and chops to a warm dish and drain the excess fat. Melt the butter in the same pan and add the chanterelles, sautéing lightly for 7 minutes. Add the chops and garlic, parsley, wine, salt and pepper to taste. Simmer covered until the chops are tender, about 1 hour. Serve with rice, mashed potatoes, or noodles. —*Carol Gass*

Pork and Chanterelles with Tomato Sauce

Serves 4 as a main course

Excellent when served over *linguine* or *fettuccine,* with a side dish of fresh vegetables.

Alternate Mushrooms:
hedgehog mushroom, boletes

¼ cup freshly grated Parmesan
    cheese
1 cup French bread crumbs
¼ cup chopped fresh parsley
Four 1-inch-thick pork chops
1 egg, beaten
3 tablespoons mild vegetable oil
1 tablespoon butter
½ pound chanterelles, chopped
1 cup tomato sauce
Salt and pepper
¼ cup dry vermouth

Mix together the Parmesan cheese, bread crumbs, and parsley. Trim the fat from the chops. Dip the chops in the egg and then in the Parmesan cheese mixture. Heat 2 tablespoons of the oil in a sauté pan or skillet and brown the chops on both sides for 4 minutes. Place the chops in a baking dish.

Heat the remaining oil and butter in a sauté pan or skillet. Cook the chanterelles for 5 minutes. Add the tomato sauce and cook 3 minutes more. Season with salt and pepper.

Pour the mushrooms and sauce over the chops in the baking dish. Add the vermouth. Bake in a preheated 350° oven until tender, about 1 hour.   —*Robert Mackler*

Chanterelles and Prawns in Cream

Serves 4 as a main course or 6 as a first course

This delicious dish is highlighted by complex flavors. Serve it as a soup or over sesame spiral pasta or brown rice as a main course.

Alternate Mushrooms:
hedgehog mushroom, milky caps

1 pound chanterelles, cut in bite size
2 tablespoons butter
20 large prawns, shelled, deveined, and split in half lenghwise
½ cup flour
Salt and pepper to taste
3 to 4 tablespoons olive oil
¼ cup chopped green onions
½ cup Dubonnet
½ cup dry white wine
5 tablespoons fresh lemon juice
1 cup heavy cream
½ cup chicken broth
Chopped fresh parsley
Freshly grated Parmesan cheese

In a sauté pan or skillet, sauté the chanterelles in the butter until only a small amount of liquid remains. Set aside.

Dust the prawns with a mixture of flour, salt, and pepper. Heat the olive oil in a sauté pan or skillet and sauté the prawns until pink and opaque. Drain on paper towels.

Put the green onions, Dubonnet, wine, lemon juice, cream, and broth in a saucepan and heat slowly for 5 to 7 minutes. Do not let the mixture boil. Remove from the heat and combine with the chanterelles and prawns. Garnish with parsley and Parmesan cheese.

—*Tom Wishing and Kathleen Cecil*

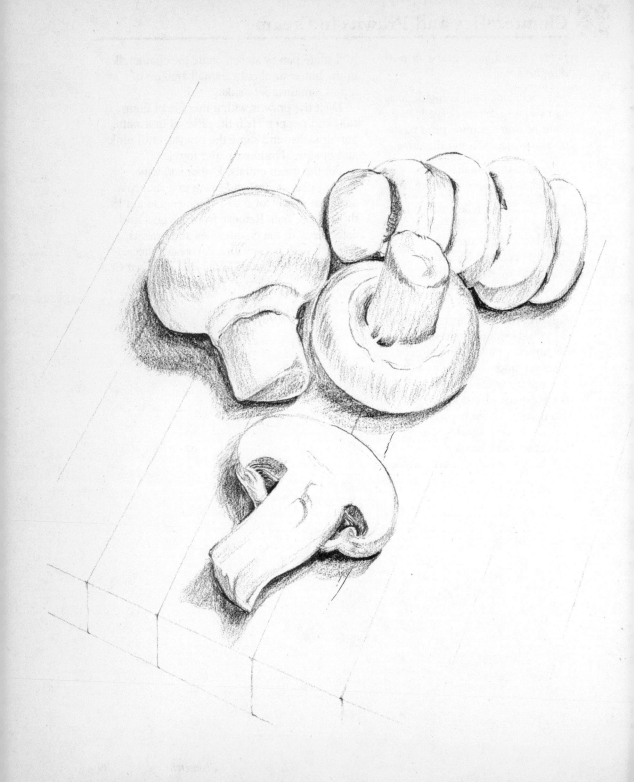

Common Store Mushroom
(*Agaricus bisporus*)

WE ADMIRE the common mushroom sold in groceries as a fine food product. It has a strong and individual flavor. It keeps well in the refrigerator. It combines with almost everything. It is available even in the worst weather, and all year long.

The common store mushroom, *Agaricus bisporus,* (also known as "commercial mushroom" and "button mushroom") was first cultivated on horse manure heaps in France in the 1700s. It is still grown this way. Until recently it was the main mushroom cultivated in the United States.

The commercial variety of *A. bisporus* was originally brown in color. In 1926, a Pennsylvania mushroom farmer found a clump of *Agaricus* with white caps in his mushroom bed. As was done with the navel orange, cultures were grown from the mutant individuals, and most of the cream-colored store mushrooms we see today are products of this chance observation.

At times mushroom growers cultivate *A. bitorquis* instead of *A. bisporus.* This is a more robust mushroom, but is otherwise difficult to distinguish from the *A. bisporus* we usually find in the marketplace.

Whole unopened buttons taste best. Once the partial veil protecting the gills has broken and the cap expands, the flesh becomes softer, cooks darker, and has a stronger taste. These more mature mushrooms do not keep as well as buttons.

A large *Agaricus* variety called "porto-bello" is sold in markets. They look like an umbrella with dark underparts. Use to complement soups and stews.

There are many kinds of wild *Agaricus.* Most resemble the cultivated species in being fleshy mushrooms that at maturity bear purple to almost black gills and a ring around the stem. Three of the most common and choice edible species are *A. campestris,* the field mushroom; *A. arvensis,* the horse mushroom; and *A. augustus,* the prince.

A. campestris is found in pastures and grasslands soon after the autumn rains. Whitish caps appear in arcs and rings as a sign of the changing season. Many people gather this more delicate mushroom as a substitute for *A. bisporus.* Beware of *A. californicus,* an upsetting look-alike for *A. campestris.*

A. campestris is especially good with eggs, most vegetables, meats, and stuffings. Pile this mushroom on top of your mozzarella-cheese pizza and bake in a hot oven, allowing the juices to flavor the cheese.

A. arvensis, the horse mushroom, is larger and more robust than the field mushroom. It also appears in grasslands, and sometimes the two species can be collected together. This mushroom is cream colored, becoming faintly yellowish in age. The smooth caps are fleshy, more than an inch thick, and stain yellow when bruised. It has a pleasant anise or almond odor when fresh.

A. augustus, the prince, is one of the meatiest and sweetest of mushrooms. The tawny brown caps may expand to a foot or more in diameter, have golden-brown scales, and smell of anise or almonds. It is equally at home in city parks and gardens or in the wild. This much-sought-after mushroom usually fruits in clumps even during the warm months. The prince can fruit several times a year and in the same location each time. *A. augustus* is more abundant in the west than on the East Coast.

You will never forget your introduction to *A. augustus* and *A. arvensis* for, raw or cooked, their odors, flavors, and textures are special. Try placing pizza ingredients inside the inverted cap of one of these mushrooms to surprise your friends. Or smother steaks or chops with thick slabs of mushrooms sautéed in butter and freshly ground pepper. The caps are thick enough to be sliced and baked with olive oil and your favorite herbs.

A Word About Purchasing Commercial Store Mushrooms

Check newspapers for sales of fresh mushrooms. Select those in prime condition, with closed caps. Some markets have large mushrooms especially selected for stuffing.

Cleaning

Little water is required for the cleaning of store-bought mushrooms or of field specimens if gathered carefully. Older ones may be fragile and difficult to clean without cracking. A soft brush is useful. Avoid soaking, for the gills retain water and they will cook poorly. For best results, let them drain in a colander 15 to 30 minutes before cooking. Prepare all species of *Agaricus* in the same manner.

Cooking

A. bisporus is thought of as the universal mushroom. It may be substituted for almost any recipe in this or any other cookbook. This is one of the few mushrooms that can be eaten raw in a salad or for dips.

Thickly sliced pieces, when sautéed, may be savored as delicate hors d'oeuvres. Added to vegetarian casseroles or stews, they may simulate hunks of meat.

Preserving

You may store fresh *Agaricus* in the refrigerator for a week in an open bowl covered with waxed paper, but avoid plastic. They may also be sautéed in butter and frozen. They are surprisingly good when cut into ½- to ¾-inch slices and dried at home for later rehydration. Buttons may be pickled, spiced, or canned. Use a pressure cooker, applying fully adequate time, heat, and pressure, when canning them. Botulism is a serious risk when mushrooms are canned at home.

Agaricus arvensis, the horse mushroom

Chicken Liver Mousse

Serves 6 to 8 as an appetizer

An attractive centerpiece for your buffet table. Serve on a bed of leafy greens.

Alternate Mushrooms:
boletes

½ pound chicken livers
4 tablespoons butter
1 tablespoon brandy
1 small onion, minced
½ pound common store
   mushrooms
½ cup plus 1 tablespoon port
   wine
2 tablespoons soft butter
Salt to taste
Freshly ground white pepper
Pinch of dried marjoram
1 envelope (1 tablespoon) plain
   gelatin
½ cup beef broth

In a sauté pan or skillet, sauté the livers in 2 tablespoons of the butter for 7 minutes. The livers should be slightly pink inside. Remove the livers to a bowl with a slotted spoon and pour the brandy into the pan. Continue to cook, scraping all the flavors from the pan. Pour it over the livers.

In the same pan, sauté the onion in the remaining 2 tablespoons of the butter for 2 to 3 minutes. Add the mushrooms and sauté for 5 minutes. Remove from the heat and add 1 tablespoon of the port wine.

Purée the liver, onion, and mushroom mixture in a blender or food processor. Add the soft butter and seasonings.

In a small bowl, sprinkle the gelatin over the broth and remaining port wine and let it stand without mixing for 3 minutes. Heat the gelatin mixture and stir until the gelatin is dissolved. Blend into the liver mixture. Pour into an oiled 4-cup mold and refrigerate for 4 to 5 hours or until firm.

—Bea Aker

Marinated Mushrooms and Artichokes

Serves 4 as a first course

1 pound baby artichokes,
   trimmed, or two
   9-ounce packages thawed
   frozen artichoke hearts
1½ cups water
1 cup cider vinegar
½ cup olive oil
1 garlic clove, quartered
1½ teaspoons minced fresh
   thyme, or ½ teaspoon dried
   thyme
1½ teaspoons minced fresh
   tarragon, or ½ teaspoon dried
   tarragon
1 bay leaf
1 pound small common store
   mushrooms
1 red bell pepper, seeded,
   deveined, and cut into strips
1 teaspoon salt
½ teaspoon ground black pepper
Chopped fresh parsley

Place the artichokes in ¼ cup of the water. Cover and bring to a boil. Reduce heat and simmer for 5 to 8 minutes, or until tender. Drain and cool.

In a large bowl, combine the remaining water, vinegar, olive oil, garlic, herbs, artichokes, mushrooms, red pepper, salt, and pepper. Toss and refrigerate overnight. Sprinkle with parsley when ready to serve.

—*Louise Freedman*

Spaghetti Squash with Mushroom Sauce

Serves 4 as a side dish

An unusual and interesting way to serve spaghetti squash. Double the recipe to serve as a vegetarian main dish.

Alternate Mushroom: shiitake

6 tablespoons butter
½ medium-sized yellow onion
1 large garlic clove, minced
½ pound common store
    mushrooms, sliced
Minced fresh oregano and basil
    to taste
One 2-pound spaghetti squash
Salt
Freshly grated Romano or
    Parmesan cheese

Melt the butter in a sauté pan or skillet. Sauté the onion and garlic over medium heat until translucent. Add the sliced mushrooms, oregano, and basil, and cook until most of the moisture from the mushrooms has evaporated. Set aside.

Slice the squash lengthwise and scrape out the seeds. (You can bake and eat these seeds like pumpkin seeds.) Place the halves in a large covered pot with 1 inch of boiling water and cook for 20 minutes. They may be placed cut side up or down. You do not want to overcook the squash because the strands of the flesh become mushy, so be sure the interior remains firm. Drain the squash and separate the circular strands of the "spaghetti" from the skin of the squash with a fork. The strands should remain slightly crunchy.

Heat the mushroom sauce. Empty the strands of squash into a heated serving dish. Mix in the mushroom sauce, adding salt to taste. Top with grated cheese and serve.

—*Dr. Bradford Beebe*

Fettuccine with Zucchini and Mushrooms

Serves 6 as a main course

The perfect dish for your vegetarian friends—and it's simple to prepare.

Alternate Mushroom:
shaggy parasol mushroom

1 pound common store mushrooms, thinly sliced
5 tablespoons butter
1½ pounds zucchini, cut into julienne strips
1 cup sour cream
1 tablespoon olive oil
1 pound *fettuccine*
¾ cup freshly grated Parmesan cheese or more
Salt to taste
¼ teaspoon cayenne
½ cup minced fresh Italian parsley

In a large saucepan sauté the mushrooms in the butter over moderate heat for 2 minutes. Add the zucchini. Cook until the zucchini is tender but slightly crisp. Allow to cool somewhat, then stir in the sour cream.

Add the olive oil to a large amount of boiling salted water, then add the pasta and cook it until *al dente*. Drain the pasta in a large colander. Add the pasta to the pan of zucchini and mushrooms. Sprinkle with the Parmesan cheese, salt, cayenne, and parsley and toss gently with a wooden fork, lifting the pasta and combining the mixture well.

Serve with additional Parmesan cheese, if you like.
—*Toby Freedman*

Flambéed Lamb Kidneys

Serves 4 as a main course

A lovely, rich dish for a winter's night.

Alternate Mushroom:
shaggy parasol mushroom

8 lamb kidneys
2 tablespoons butter
1 tablespoon mild vegetable oil
½ pound common store mushrooms, sliced
2 teaspoons shallots or green onions, chopped
⅓ cup warm brandy
Salt and pepper to taste
½ teaspoon dry mustard
¾ cup heavy cream

Trim the fat from the kidneys and cut them into slices.

Heat the butter and oil in a sauté pan or skillet. Add the kidney slices, mushrooms, and shallots. Sauté for 4 to 5 minutes or until the kidneys turn brown but are still pink at the center. Add the warm brandy. Ignite. When the flames burn out, sprinkle with salt and pepper. Stir in the dry mustard and heavy cream. Cook until the cream is hot, and serve over rice or noodles.
—*Cil Black and Bill Thele*

Ceviche

Serves 4 as a first course

This recipe is prepared in advance to be served cold. You may substitute tuna or red snapper for the scallops.

Alternate Mushroom:
enoki

1 pound bay scallops
¾ cup fresh lime or lemon juice
1 large onion, sliced
1 small hot green chili, chopped
½ pound small firm common
    store mushrooms
½ teaspoon ground pepper
1½ teaspoons minced fresh
    oregano
2 tablespoons tarragon vinegar
2 medium tomatoes, chopped
½ cup virgin olive oil

Place the scallops in a glass dish with the lime or lemon juice and cover. Let them stand 2 hours; drain. Mix all the remaining ingredients, except the oil, and blend with the scallops. Add the oil. Allow to chill for several hours before serving (but not more than 12 hours). Serve cold in cocktail glasses.

—Kitchen Magic with Mushrooms

Fennel and Mushrooms

Serves 4 to 5 as a side dish

A good dish to serve around Christmastime when fennel appears in the marketplace.

Alternate Mushroom:
oyster mushroom

½ head fennel, cut into small
    strips about ½ by 1½ inches
4 tablespoons butter
¼ cup water
1 pound small to medium
    common store mushrooms,
    halved
Salt and pepper to taste
½ cup sour cream
Fennel leaves

In a saucepan, cook the fennel in 2 tablespoons of the butter and the water for 3 minutes or until tender. Melt the remaining 2 tablespoons of butter in a sauté pan or skillet and sauté the mushrooms for about 3 minutes. Sprinkle with salt and pepper.

Drain the fennel and add to the mushrooms. Stir in the sour cream. Serve at once, topped with the chopped fennel leaves.

—*Margaret Waterhouse*

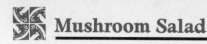# Mushroom Salad

Serves 4 as a first course

The common store mushroom is one of the few mushrooms that can be eaten raw. The prince and horse mushrooms are excellent alternatives.

1 pound small common store
    mushrooms, sliced
2 cups water
1 tablespoon fresh lemon juice
3 to 4 celery sticks, sliced
    diagonally
2 tablespoons chopped fresh
    parsley
4 to 5 green onions, cut
    lengthwise into 1-inch strips
1 small jar pimientos, drained
    and minced
½ teaspoon capers, drained
¼ cup virgin olive oil
1 tablespoon tarragon vinegar
1 teaspoon anchovy paste
½ garlic clove, crushed
Ground pepper to taste
Dash of Tabasco sauce
Lettuce leaves

Dip the mushrooms into a mixture of the water and lemon juice. Place in a colander to drain. Mix the celery, parsley, green onions, pimientos, capers, and mushrooms in a mixing bowl.

In a pint jar, mix the olive oil, vinegar, anchovy paste, garlic, pepper, and Tabasco. Pour this over the ingredients in the mixing bowl; remove and discard the garlic. Toss carefully, making sure to coat each mushroom, but avoid leaving a pool of liquid in the bottom of the bowl.

Serve on lettuce leaves in individual bowls.

    —Kitchen Magic with Mushrooms

Tortière

A wonderful French-Canadian meat, potato, and mushroom tart that can be made with the common store mushroom, blewit, or shaggy parasol.

Savory Pastry

1½ cups unbleached all-purpose
    flour
½ teaspoon salt
½ cup (1 stick) butter
2 tablespoons vinegar
4 to 5 tablespoons ice water

Filling

3 medium red potatoes, peeled
½ pound lean ground pork
¼ pound ground beef round
1 garlic clove, pressed
1 pound common store
    mushrooms, thinly sliced
1 cup coarsely chopped red
    onion
¼ teaspoon ground dried sage
1 teaspoon chopped fresh basil
¼ teaspoon chopped fresh
    rosemary
1 teaspoon salt
½ teaspoon freshly ground black
    pepper
1 cup water
1 egg

1 egg, slightly beaten with
    1 tablespoon water
Slices of sour pickle
1 bunch fresh watercress

To make the pastry, combine the flour and salt in a mixing bowl. Cut the butter into the flour with a pastry cutter or 2 knives until the mixture is crumbly. Add the vinegar and water and work the dough into a ball. Sprinkle it with flour, wrap it in plastic wrap, and place it in the refrigerator for 1 hour before making the crusts.

To make the filling, boil the potatoes in salted water for 20 minutes or until tender; drain. Cut the potatoes into coarse pieces and whip with a whisk. Set aside.

In a large sauté pan or skillet, combine the pork, beef, and garlic and sauté until browned. Remove any excess fat and add the mushrooms and the onion. Sauté 2 minutes and add the sage, basil, rosemary, salt, pepper, and water. Cover and simmer for 10 minutes. Remove from the heat and stir in the whipped potatoes and egg. Cool.

To make the crust, use a fluted 10-inch tart pan with a removable bottom. Roll out half of the crust and fit into a tart pan. Trim the edges and fill it with the meat and mushroom filling. Roll out the the other half and cover the tart; trim and seal the edges. Generously brush the top with the egg-water mixture. Bake in a preheated 350° oven for 30 minutes, or until the crust is golden brown.

Remove the tart from the pan while slightly warm and place on a serving platter. Make a ring of pickle slices and watercress sprigs around the tart.   — *Shea Moss, from* If You Can't Eat Your Mushroom Take It Dancing

Piutipana

Serves 4 as a main dish

Piutipana is a Danish pork stew with mushrooms, tomatoes, and cream. Beef jerky is used for flavoring.

Alternate Mushroom:
hedgehog mushroom

1 pound pork loin, cut into strips
Flour
¼ pound bacon, cut into 1-inch pieces
½ cup chopped onion
½ pound common store mushrooms, sliced
½ pound tomatoes, peeled, seeded, and chopped
2 to 3 pieces beef jerky (optional)
¾ cup sour cream
2 tablespoons dry sherry
¼ cup heavy cream
Salt and pepper

Dredge the pork strips in the flour. In a sauté pan or skillet, sauté the bacon for a few minutes. Then add the pork strips and brown lightly for 10 minutes. Remove the pork strips and bacon with a slotted spoon. Add the onion and mushrooms to the pan and sauté for 5 minutes. Add the tomatoes and beef jerky. Simmer for 15 minutes or so. Return the pork strips and bacon to the pan.

Add the sour cream, sherry, and cream, and stir. Heat briefly. Do not boil. Correct the seasoning and remove the jerky, if used. Serve with buttered noodles. —*Roma Wagner*

Chicken Livers and Mushrooms Flambé

Serves 6 as a main course

Chicken livers should be cooked quickly so that they remain pink and juicy inside.

Alternate Mushroom:
chanterelle

1½ pounds chicken livers
½ cup milk
1 cup flour
½ teaspoon ground pepper
½ teaspoon salt
¼ teaspoon ground nutmeg
⅛ teaspoon cayenne
3 tablespoons olive oil
7 tablespoons butter
4 to 5 shallots or green onions,
    chopped
1½ pounds common store
    mushrooms, sliced
¼ cup chopped fresh parsley
Juice of ½ lemon
½ cup brandy, heated

The day before serving, place the livers in a mixing bowl and pour the milk over them. Stir well and refrigerate overnight.

Drain the chicken livers; discard the milk. Allow the livers to drain well in a colander. Place the flour in a paper bag. Add the pepper, salt, nutmeg, and cayenne. Add a few livers at a time and shake the bag to coat the livers. Heat the olive oil and 3 tablespoons of the butter in a large sauté pan or skillet. Add the floured livers and sauté for 3 to 5 minutes or until brown and crusted but still pink inside.

In a separate skillet, sauté the shallots in the remaining 4 tablespoons of butter for about 3 minutes. Add the mushooms, parsley, and lemon juice. Blend and heat thoroughly. Combine the mushroom-shallot mixture with the chicken livers. Poor the heated brandy over and ignite. Mix well until the flames subside. Serve immediately.

—Kitchen Magic with Mushrooms

Mushroom Bread

Makes 1 loaf

A nutritious bread made with
sautéed mushrooms, honey, soy
sauce, and yogurt.

4 tablespoons butter
1 medium onion, minced
1 pound common store
    mushrooms, minced
3 tablespoons soy sauce
1 cup warm water
1 package active dry yeast
2 tablespoons honey
1½ teaspoons salt
2 tablespoons plain yogurt
5 to 6 cups unbleached all-
    purpose flour

Melt the butter in a sauté pan or skillet and
sauté the onion until translucent. Add the
mushrooms and cook until all the liquid
evaporates. Add the soy sauce and cook until
the mushrooms become brown. Let them cool.

Pour the warm water into a large mixing
bowl. Sprinkle the yeast on top of the water.
Add the honey and let it stand without mixing
for 10 minutes, allowing the honey to react with
the yeast.

Add the salt, cool mushroom mixture, and
yogurt to the mixing bowl and stir well. Slowly
add the flour. When the dough becomes too
difficult to mix with a spoon, use your hands.
Continue to add the flour until the dough
becomes pliable and can be made into a ball.
Cover with a towel and let it rise in a warm
place for 2 to 3 hours or until doubled in size.

Knead the dough on a floured board,
counting 50 times, adding flour whenever the
dough becomes sticky. Grease a 9-by-5-inch
loaf pan and neatly place the dough in the
bottom. Let it rise again for about ½ hour.

Bake in a preheated 400° oven for about 20
minutes. As soon as the crust turns slightly
brown, brush the top with warm water. Lower
the oven temperature to 300° and bake until
the crust becomes brown all over, about 15
minutes more. Remove from the pan and cool
on a baking rack.   *—Louise Freedman*

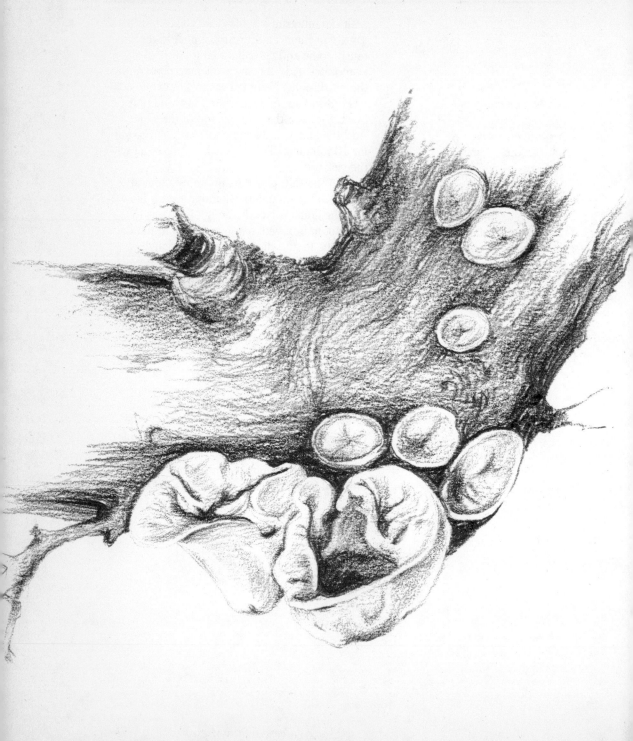

Ear Mushrooms:
Cloud Ear (Auricularia auricula),
Wood Ear (A. polytricha)

TWO SPECIES of *Auricularia*, a group of jelly fungi, are often used in Asian cuisine. Both are sold dried in Asian markets and are reasonably priced compared to many wild or cultivated mushrooms. For culinary purposes, they are identical.

Auricularia polytricha is variously called "wood ear," "tree ear," "black fungus," or *muk nge*. The dried ear-shaped cap is medium sized, dull in texture, and dark brown to black. The wavy lower surface has a contrasting powdery gray color. The stem is absent or rudimentary. It has no gills. It is a native of Asia and some Pacific Ocean islands in humid climates. Most major Asian countries successfully cultivate *A. polytricha* today. They are found fresh sold in many produce markets.

These fungi are used for their crisp, snappy texture and their color rather than their taste. The Chinese regularly add *A. polytricha* to dishes because they think it improves breathing, circulation, and well-being. And they may be correct. Recent studies of the medicinal effects of *Auricularia polytricha* have identified a chemical that tends to inhibit blood clotting. Since blood vessel diseases, strokes, and heart attacks are associated with clotting, perhaps moderate ingestion of this mushroom as food may indeed confer long life and good health on its users.

Auricularia auricula, "cloud ear," "Judas' ear," or *yung nge,* is a smaller fungus, with a brown to black cap surface, and is dull brown underneath. *A. auricula* is not restricted to Asian countries. It is found growing on dead wood worldwide. Plan to pay more for it than for *A. polytricha.*

Both fungi are imported dried from Asia packed in plastic bags. Store the mushrooms in well-covered heavy plastic or glass containers.

You get your money's worth when you buy this fungus, especially *A. polytricha*. A wood ear will rehydrate in hot water in 15 to 20 minutes, and swell two to five times its original size. It will look like an enormous, swollen, shiny black ear. Only two or three pieces are needed for four servings.

Cleaning

After reconstitution in warm water, clean under running water with light finger pressure to remove debris. Cut off any fibrous material adhering to the base of the mushroom.

Cooking

These mushrooms are usually sliced in ¼-inch strips for cooking. Cook them for only a short time. In fact, if allowed to stand with food for any length of time, these mushrooms lose their firmness. For soups, stir-fried dishes, or salads, add such slices as the last stage of food preparation.

Preserving

This fungus will not store well after rehydration. Keep it dry in insect-proof containers.

Ma-Po Tofu

Serves 6 as a first course

An unusual soup containing exotic Chinese ingredients. The Chinese-style tofu is the firm variety. The Szechwan peppercorns are not related to our black pepper. They will last for a long time if sealed in a glass jar. The fermented black beans, hot bean sauce, and Asian sesame oil are available in Chinese markets.

2 packages Chinese-style tofu, cut into small cubes

½ teaspoon Szechwan peppercorns

3 to 4 wood ear mushrooms

2 to 3 large fresh or dried *shiitake* mushrooms

1 large pork chop, fat left on

3 tablespoons minced fresh ginger

2 tablespoons minced garlic

1 teaspoon fermented black beans, rinsed, drained, and chopped

1½ teaspoons hot bean sauce

3 tablespoons oil

1 cup chicken broth or water

2 tablespoons cornstarch

¼ cup water

1 tablespoon soy sauce

2 green onions, including the tops, cut into 1-inch lengths

1 tablespoon Asian sesame oil

Place the tofu in a mixing bowl and cover with boiling water for 1 to 2 minutes. Drain. Heat and stir the peppercorns in a dry wok until they begin to smoke and smell of pepper. In a mortar, grind the peppercorns into a fine powder. Soak the wood ear mushrooms in hot water for 15 to 20 minutes. Drain and slice into small sections. If using dried *shiitakes,* soak for 20 minutes in hot water. Drain and chop into matchstick pieces. Slice the pork into small pieces.

Mix together the ginger, garlic, beans, and bean sauce. Heat the oil in a wok and stir-fry the pork until the color changes. Remove to a plate with a slotted spoon. Quickly stir-fry the garlic mixture. Add to the meat. Let the wok cool a little and add the broth or water. Add the drained tofu and cook gently until the liquid reduces somewhat. Stir in the *shiitake* mushrooms, wood ears, and pork and garlic mixture.

In a small bowl, mix the cornstarch, water, and soy sauce together. If necessary, adjust thickening. Add the onions and sesame oil, and serve immediately.   —*Helen Studebaker*

Sweetbreads with Two Kinds of Mushrooms

Serves 6 as a main course

An exquisite dish blending many flavors with subtlety. Serve with white or brown rice, or pasta. Chardonnay or champagne will complete this meal.

Alternate Mushroom:
substitute *shiitakes* for ear mushrooms

2 pounds sweetbreads
Vinegar
1 bay leaf
3 allspice berries
1 small handful dried wood ear
   mushrooms
4 tablespoons butter
1 large sweet onion, sliced
¼ cup brandy
½ cup dry white wine
½ pound cooked ham, cut into
   ½-by-½-by-2-inch slices
1 pound common store
   mushrooms, sliced
¼ cup heavy cream
¼ cup chopped fresh parsley

Soak the sweetbreads in cold water to cover for 1 hour, changing the water 2 or 3 times. Drain and place in a deep pot. Measure out cold water to cover, then add 1 tablespoon vinegar per quart of water. Add the bay leaf and allspice. Bring to a boil, reduce heat, and simmer for 15 minutes.

Drain the sweetbreads and plunge them into cold water for 5 minutes. Drain again. With fingers remove the dark veins and thick membrane from the sweetbreads.

Soak the wood ears in hot water to cover for 15 to 20 minutes. Squeeze the mushrooms dry and cut to bite size.

In a large sauté pan or skillet, heat the butter until foamy. Brown the sweetbreads on all sides. Add the onion and cook rapidly until the meat is tender. Heat the brandy gently and pour over the sweetbreads and onion. Ignite. When the flames go out, add the white wine, ham, wood ears, and store mushrooms. When these are done to taste, stir in the cream and parsley.

                              —*Carolyn Richmond*

Shrimp with Wood Ears

Serves 4 to 6 as a main course

A fragrant, well-seasoned shrimp dish with bite-sized pieces of ear mushrooms. Take care not to overcook the shrimp or the wood ears.

Alternate Mushroom:
shiitake

1 small handful dried wood ear mushrooms
1 tablespoon Asian sesame oil (available in Asian markets)
2 tablespoons peanut oil
1 to 2 garlic cloves, minced
1 teaspoon grated fresh ginger
1 pound shrimp, peeled and deveined
1 green onion, sliced
2 carrots, very thinly sliced
½ cup bamboo shoots, sliced
½ cup fresh or thawed frozen green peas
1 cup bean sprouts
3 tablespoons dry white wine
1 teaspoon soy sauce
¼ teaspoon grated lemon peel
Cilantro sprigs

Soak the wood ears in hot water to cover until soft, about 15 to 20 minutes. Squeeze the mushrooms dry and cut to bite size.

In a wok or skillet, heat the sesame and peanut oils. Add the garlic and ginger and stir over medium heat. Add the shrimp, wood ears, and green onion. Stir-fry until the shrimp are pink and opaque. Remove the mixture from the pan with a slotted spoon.

Turn the heat high and add the carrots, bamboo shoots, and green peas and stir for a minute. Add the sprouts, wine, and soy sauce. Add a little water if needed. Stir-fry for 2 minutes.

Return the shrimp mixture to the wok and stir-fry for another minute. Serve on a heated plate and garnish with grated lemon peel and whole sprigs of cilantro.   —*Lois Der*

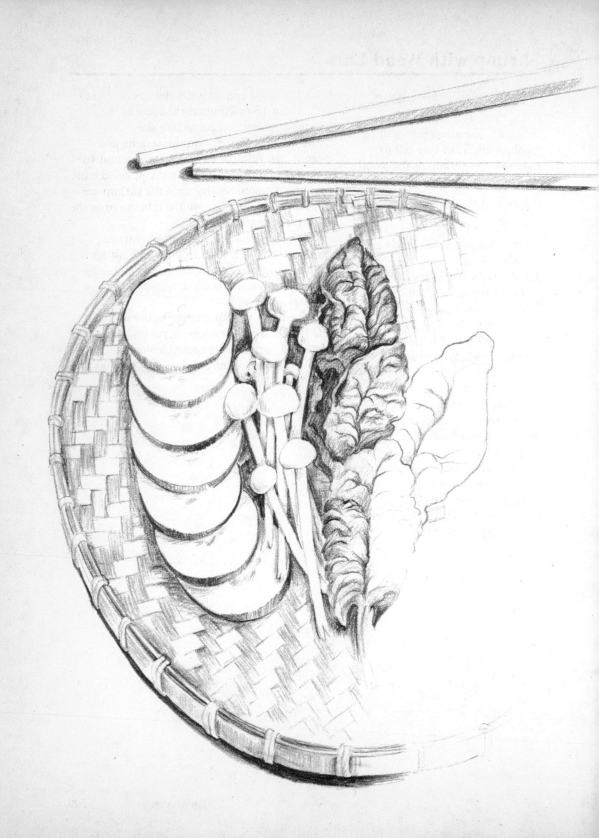

Enoki
(Flammulina velutipes)

THIS CULTIVATED introduction from Japan looks like no other mushroom. Long legged, uniformly smooth and cream colored, it resembles a bean sprout or perhaps a straightened spaghetti noodle with a tiny mushroom cap. Other common names are "golden needle," "winter mushroom," and "velvet foot." In Japan it is called *enokidake*.

The winter mushroom grows wild in North America during the fall and winter months. It is found clustered on hardwood stumps, frequently as snow is melting around it. Its appearance is totally different from that of the cultivated form. The caps are 2 to 3 inches broad, yellow to tan in color and sticky to the touch, while the stems are shorter and covered with red-brown velvet (*velutipes* means "velvet foot").

Cultivated *enoki* are sold canned and in long bottles, or packed fresh in plastic containers. Be sure to examine fresh ones carefully before buying them. They should be shiny but not slimy, and firm, not soft. The base of the clump should be clean and not decomposed. Cut the lower ½ inch or more from the bottom of the stems, which tend to be tough and fibrous.

Cleaning

Rinse before using by pouring boiling water over them.

Cooking

As a complement to almost any salad, *enokis* will add crispness and a subtle radishy flavor similar to nasturtium leaves and flowers. Eaten raw, they will leave a hint of pepper on your tongue.

Toss some into soup during the last few minutes of simmering, or drop them into stir-fried vegetable or meat dishes just before serving.

Fresh, crisp *enokis* refrigerated in their original package will keep well for about a week.

Hot and Sour Soup with Three Kinds of Mushrooms

Serves 4 to 6 as a first course

A traditional hot and sour soup that includes *enoki, shiitake,* and oyster mushrooms. Firm tofu is available in Chinese markets.

6 to 8 large fresh or dried
   shiitake mushrooms
8 cups chicken broth
1 single chicken breast, skinned,
   boned, and minced
1 teaspoon grated fresh ginger
½ cup chopped bamboo shoots
½ pound Chinese-style tofu, cut
   into cubes
1 handful oyster mushrooms, cut
   into strips
¼ pound *enoki* mushrooms
2 green onions, chopped
1 tablespoon cornstarch
¼ cup cold water
1 egg, slightly beaten
2 tablespoons soy sauce
2 tablespoons white vinegar
2 teaspoons Asian sesame oil
   (available in Asian markets)

If using dried *shiitakes,* soak them in hot water for 20 minutes. Drain. In a large pot, bring the broth to a simmer and add the chicken, ginger, and bamboo shoots. Stir the tofu into the soup. Slice the *shiitakes* and add with the oyster mushrooms to the broth. Add half the *enokis,* and the chopped green onions.

Dissolve the cornstarch in water and stir *slowly* into the simmering soup. Remove from the heat, adding the egg, soy sauce, vinegar, and sesame oil, and adjust the seasoning. Top with the remaining *enokis.*   —*Terri Woodring*

Natural Food Sandwich

Serves 2

Treat crunchy *enokis* as sprouts in this sandwich lunch.

Alternate Mushroom:
common store mushroom

1 tablespoon soy sauce
Cayenne to taste
1 large avocado, peeled and
   mashed
4 slices whole-grain bread
2 tomato slices
1 large carrot, grated
Grated Cheddar cheese
½ package *enokis,* washed and
   trimmed

Mix the soy sauce and cayenne with the mashed avocado. Place a layer of the avocado mixture on 2 slices of bread, then the tomato, grated carrot, and cheese, ending with the *enoki* mushrooms. Cover each slice with a second slice of bread. Press down and cut diagonally.
                                        —*Louise Freedman*

Fairy-Ring Mushroom
(Marasmius oreades)

THIS PETITE mushroom is a nuisance to lawn owners: its mycelium browns the grass in arcs and rings. But it redeems itself by being a fine food. A homeowner can fight back by eating the mushrooms as they periodically appear. The rings formed by *Marasmius oreades* increase in diameter with time as the fungus seeks new food. Rings may grow to many feet across. A number of studies measuring distance and growth rate have estimated that rings of the *M. oreades* are probably centuries old and hundreds of feet across. The grass inside the ring recovers, but along the borders the damage continues. The French call it *faux mousseron,* or "mushroom scythe." The fairy-ring mushroom fruits abundantly during the warm months in the eastern United States, and all year in the west after rain or periodic watering.

The flat, dry, tan to brown *Marasmius* caps are little more than 1 inch in diameter. The centers are raised and dome shaped. The widely separated buff-colored gills throw off many white spores. The odor of these mushrooms is agreeable. When waterlogged and aged, however, they acquire a fetid and disagreeable smell. It only takes one or two of these to foul a batch of dried mushrooms. Sun-dried specimens found on the lawn are safe, but not as good as mature caps dried at home. (Remember: do not try to identify mushrooms without the help of an expert.)

Cleaning

Remove the fibrous stems with scissors and discard. They are too tough to eat. Insects seldom attack these mushrooms. Clean the tops under water with your fingers.

Cooking

The flavor and aroma of *M. oreades* are out of proportion to its size. Added fresh to soups, ragouts, and stews, it confers a definite, somewhat sweet taste. This sweet quality also enhances the taste of cookies. It is excellent sautéed in butter with onions. Surprise your friends and family with a subtle change in flavor by adding this tasty and fragrant mushroom to your favorite soup.

The caps are quite firm and tolerate long cooking. To prepare for use where shorter cooking times are called for, simmer them beforehand for 15 minutes in water with butter and lemon juice.

Preserving

This mushroom is often dried before use, although it is delicious fresh. The caps are thin and dry quickly. String them on a thread with a button on the bottom and hang in a warm place. One of the unique characteristics of *M. oreades* is its amazing ability to rapidly take up water to resume its original texture, appearance, and taste. You needn't soak it prior to adding it to such foods as soups or stews. Just drop it into your pot.

 # Rice Pilaf with Fairy-Ring Mushrooms

Serves 4 as a side dish

Alternate Mushrooms:
candy cap, chanterelle, common store mushroom

5 tablespoons butter
1 cup fairy-ring mushrooms
1 cup long-grain rice
2 cups hot beef broth
Dash of cayenne
Salt and pepper to taste

Melt the butter in a heavy sauté pan or skillet and sauté the mushrooms for 5 minutes. Add the rice and cook for another 3 minutes. Stir in the beef broth. Adjust the flavor by adding the cayenne, salt, and pepper. Cover and simmer about 15 minutes or until the rice is soft and fuffy. Remove the lid and continue to cook for a few more minutes.　　　—*Louise Freedman*

Fairy-Ring Mushroom Soup

Serves 4 as first course

A great way to experience this small but strongly flavored mushroom.

Alternate Mushroom:
candy cap

1 cup fresh or dried fairy-ring mushrooms (soaking these mushrooms is not necessary)
2 large shallots or green onions, minced
3 tablespoons butter
2 tablespoons flour
2 cups beef or chicken broth
2 cups half and half
1 thyme sprig
1 teaspoon Tabasco sauce
Cayenne
Salt
¼ cup dry sherry

If using fresh mushrooms, cook them with the shallots and butter in a heavy soup pot for 3 minutes. If using dried mushrooms, add about ½ cup of water to the pot with the butter and shallots. Add the flour, stir a minute or two, and whisk in the broth. Add the half and half, thyme, Tabasco sauce, cayenne, and salt to taste.

Simmer the soup over low heat for 10 minutes. Do not allow it to boil. Add the sherry just before serving. *—Louise Freedman*

 # Fairy-Ring Cookies

The sweetness of the fairy-ring mushroom enhances the flavor of cookies.

Your favorite sugar cookie recipe, without the flavoring
1 cup dried fairy-ring mushroom caps, minced
½ teaspoon almond extract

Mix the cookies according to the recipe. Add the mushrooms and almond extract. Bake according to the recipe directions.

—Kitchen Magic with Mushrooms

Hedgehog Mushroom
(Hydnum repandum)

MUSHROOMS with teeth? As a matter of fact, yes. Nothing intimidating, mind you, but these mushrooms do have small toothlike projections rather than gills on their lower cap surfaces. The tooth fungi, also known as "hedgehog" and "sweet tooth," appear in a variety of forms. Some grow as shelves on trees. Most are found on the ground. Colorful ones decorate the forest floor with their white, buff, red, orange-brown, blue, and purple caps. Several of the brightly colored wood varieties are used for dyeing woolen yarns. Only two kinds, *Hydnum repandum* and *H. umbilicatum,* are commonly eaten. Both are late bloomers, tending to appear in January along the Pacific Coast after other edible mushrooms have stopped fruiting. In the east they appear from July to November.

Hydnum repandum is large, fleshy, buff colored, and found occasionally in groups under conifers or hardwood trees. White teethlike structures bear the spores. In a young specimen the teeth are firm. This is a good way to determine its age. When young, it has a mild, fresh odor, and it tastes best.

Hydnum umbilicatum, sometimes called the belly-button mushroom, is found in the dense undergrowth under rhododendron bushes and other forest shrubbery. It is smaller and darker than *H. repandum.* The cap is an inch or less in diameter and is depressed in the middle like a belly button. It romps around through the leaves in troops. Clean as you would *H. repandum.*

Tiny *H. umbilicatum* is delicious sautéed with butter until brown. This is a chewy mushroom with a prominent flavor enjoyed by children who won't eat most other wild mushrooms. Sauté quantities of these mushrooms to smother steaks and chops or pile onto toast or crackers.

H. umbilicatum freezes well after being sautéed. Remember, only the young and firm are worth preserving.

A number of varieties of gorgeously delicate, white, beardlike mushrooms are occasionally stumbled on in the woods. These are in the genus *Hericium.* They grow only on wood, sometimes under the bark of large fallen logs. Wash them in running water and inspect for insects.

They may be prepared in any way, even served uncooked in salads, but should be used only when they are white, brittle, and young. Try combining them with onions, peas and a little soy sauce after first sautéing the mushroom in butter. *Hericium erinaceus* is now being cultivated in the United States, where it is called "bear's head" or "pom-pom blanc," and in China, where it is known as "monkey head."

Cleaning

Brush their surfaces. Check the toothed undercaps for uninvited guests, and cut off damaged ends. Spread on paper towels to dry.

H. repandum requires light brushing with a little water to clean debris from the cap. Try not to wet the underside. Blot dry on paper towels.

Cooking

The hedgehog mushroom has been described by some as having a mild chanterelle flavor. The color is similar to the white chanterelle. When older, they tend to be darker and taste bitter, so use only firm blond specimens. Their best use is in casseroles.

Preserving

If you pickle *H. repandum* in vinegar and spices, it will last for a few weeks. It can be sautéed in butter and frozen.

Drying toothed mushrooms is not advised. The mushrooms become fragile and grainy, and their teeth fall out. When reconstituted in water they are tough and tasteless.

Vegetarian Pickled Herring

Serves 4 as an appetizer

A Swedish recipe using the hedgehog mushroom to simulate herring. It will keep in the refrigerator for 1 week.

1 to 1½ pounds hedgehog
    mushrooms
1 bay leaf
10 allspice berries
1 onion, cut into rings
½ cup water
3½ teaspoons distilled white
    vinegar
5 tablespoons sugar

Place the mushrooms in a saucepan with water to cover. Bring to a boil, then reduce the heat and cook for 3 minutes. Drain and cut them into 3-inch slices. Place in a glass container together with the bay leaf, allspice, and onion rings.

In a large saucepan cook the water, vinegar, and sugar together for about 2 minutes and pour over the spices and mushrooms. Let cool and serve.   *—Carla Sundström*

Hedgehogs and Vegetables

Serves 4 as a side dish

A quick, simple vegetable dish. Other mushrooms can be substituted in this recipe.

4 tablespoons butter
2 to 3 hedgehog mushrooms,
    sliced
1 onion, sliced
2 carrots, sliced
6 green onions, cut into tops and
    heads
1 zucchini, sliced
1 small head cauliflower, cut into
    florets
1 tablespoon beef concentrate
½ teaspoon sugar
Salt to taste
2 tablespoons water
Freshly ground black pepper
    (optional)

In a large sauté pan or skillet melt the butter and sauté the mushrooms and onion for 5 minutes. Add the other vegetables and toss gently. Add the beef concentrate, sugar, salt, and water. Cover and simmer until the vegetables are just barely *al dente*. Grind black pepper on top and serve on white rice.

    —Kitchen Magic with Mushrooms

Scalloped Hedgehogs

Serves 4 as a side dish

The gentle flavors of hedgehogs and potatoes combined with the smoky flavor of bacon make this an interesting dish.

Alternate Mushroom:
common store mushroom

4 medium red potatoes, peeled
    and thinly sliced
¼ cup heavy cream
1 pound hedgehog mushrooms,
    sliced (including stem)
¼ cup chopped fresh chives or
    green onions
Paprika to taste
¼ cup milk
¼ cup freshly grated Parmesan
    cheese
4 bacon slices, chopped

In a buttered casserole dish, place half of the sliced potatoes and the cream. Add the sliced hedgehogs and cover with the remaining potatoes. Cover and bake in a preheated 375° oven for 25 minutes. Add the chives, paprika, and milk. Sprinkle with the cheese and bacon. Return to the oven, uncovered this time, and bake at 375° for another 20 minutes.

—*Al Cattalini*

Breast of Veal with Hedgehog Mushrooms

Serve 4 to 6 as a main course

A dish that may be cooked ahead of time and reheated. Serve over egg noodles. Dried *porcini* are a tasty substitute for the hedgehog mushrooms in this recipe. Soak them in half water and half dry red wine.

Salt and pepper to taste
One 3-pound breast of veal, cut
   into single ribs
½ cup flour
7 tablespoons mild vegetable oil
2 tablespoons butter
8 garlic cloves, minced
1 large onion, minced
2 tablespoons tomato paste
¾ cup beef broth or more
1 bay leaf
½ teaspoon dried thyme
3 allspice berries
1½ pounds hedgehog
   mushrooms, sliced
2 tablespoons chopped fresh
   parsley

Salt and pepper the ribs, then pat with the flour. Brown in 5 tablespoons of the oil in a Dutch oven and set aside.

Wipe the pot clean and add the butter and the remaining 2 tablespoons of oil. Cook the garlic and onion for 2 minutes. Add the tomato paste, broth, bay leaf, thyme, and allspice, along with the mushrooms and the ribs.

Cover and cook over low heat for 1½ to 2 hours. If the sauce becomes too thick, add more beef broth. Remove the bay leaf after 30 minutes of cooking. Sprinkle on the parsley just before serving.   *—George Damron IV*

Honey Mushroom
(Armillaria mellea)

THE HONEYLIKE color of this white-spored gilled mushroom inspired its common name.

This mushroom is very abundant. Variable in appearance, returning each year in many shapes and colors, what we call *Armillaria mellea* (also known as the "oak mushroom") may represent more than one species of mushroom. The caps can be red-brown to tan, smooth or scaled, with tan or pale brown fibrils. They may be small, rounded, and bell-like, or flat and fully expanded. They appear as individuals or in troops of hundreds. They are enjoyed worldwide.

Their partial veils are frequently rudimentary or disappear early. The veil tissues are unique in this genus. The annular ring extends outward somewhat like the nodes on a bamboo stem.

The honey mushroom grows both on dead wood and on living plants. It is capable of attacking and killing many kinds of trees, especially oaks. We have seen hundreds of caps erupting in clumps from the trunk and roots of a single tree. The mycelia of this organism may be compressed into a network of shiny black rootlike filaments called *rhizomorphs,* meaning "shaped like roots." These strands extend along tree trunks, under rocks, and follow roots underground searching for new food sources. For instance, they will consume all the plants of the cabbage family they can reach.

Logs in moist forest environments may glow at night with a cool, blue-green emanation called "fox fire." This phenomenon is caused by a chemical produced by the mycelia of the honey mushroom.

Certain orchids depend on *A. mellea* to wet-nurse their seeds until they erupt from the ground to begin photosynthesizing their own sugars. The orchid seedlings must grow underground for several years, during which time this fungus provides them with basic nutrients for survival.

Those who collect the honey mushroom for food prefer solid, young, unopened buttons. When cooked, it is firm and granular. To some it is moderately sweet in flavor, but its edibility is marred for others by a mild bitter aftertaste and a somewhat gelatinous surface. Occasional incidents of gastric upsets have been reported with this mushroom, so caution should be used when it is first eaten.

Cleaning

Brush debris from the caps and gills under running water. Only the caps are used, for the stems are fibrous and inedible.

Cooking

This mushroom is admired in many countries of the world for its firm meaty texture. Most recipes call for combining it with other ingredients, rather than preparing it alone. It can be substituted in any basic recipe. Because of its dense consistency, it tolerates long cooking without losing its shape. For those people who experience a slightly bitter aftertaste, it is advised to parboil the caps for 5 minutes and to discard the water.

Preserving

When dried and reconstituted, the honey mushroom is quite agreeable in soups, stews, and mushroom loaves. Many people pickle the buttons in their favorite spices for immediate or later use.

Honey Mushroom Salad

Serves 2 to 3 as a salad

A robust way of treating the honey mushroom, using black sesame seeds for flavoring. Black sesame seeds can be found in Asian markets.

Alternate Mushroom: shiitake

¾ cup water
Pinch of salt
1 pound honey mushroom caps
¼ cup black sesame seeds
6 tablespoons mild vegetable oil
5 tablespoons rice wine vinegar
    or fresh lemon juice
¼ cup dry sherry
2 tablespoons soy sauce
1 small head nappa cabbage, cut
    into very fine strips

Bring the water, salt, and mushroom caps to a boil in a saucepan and cook gently for 8 to 10 minutes. Remove from the heat and drain well.

Toast the sesame seeds in a dry skillet, stirring until fragrant; be careful not to burn them. Mix the sesame seeds with the oil, vinegar, sherry, and soy sauce. Toss the mixture with the mushrooms and refrigerate until slightly chilled. Serve on a bed of cabbage.
                                        —*Loraine Berry*

Pork Stew with Honey Mushrooms

Serves 4 as a main course

This recipe was developed by Loraine's father, who introduced her to the joy of foraging for wild mushrooms in the forests of southern Michigan.

Alternate Mushrooms:
black saddle mushrooom, hedgehog mushroom

2 tablespoons peanut oil
2½ pounds lean pork, cubed
3 medium onions, coarsely chopped
3 cups water or more
1 to 1½ pounds honey mushroom caps (mature caps have more flavor)
3 cups ¼-inch-thick celery slices
½ cup soy sauce (or to taste)
2 tablespoons flour mixed with ½ cup cold water
½ pound bean sprouts
Ground pepper to taste

Heat the oil in a heavy pot and sear the pork cubes, removing them as they brown. When all are browned, return them to the pot and add the chopped onions and the water. Cover and simmer gently for 30 minutes. Add the mushroom caps and more water if necessary and simmer for 20 minutes longer. Add the celery, soy sauce, and the flour-water mixture. Stir and cook for 2 to 3 minutes. The celery should be cooked but should remain slightly crisp. Add the bean sprouts. Cover and remove from heat. In about 5 minutes the bean sprouts will be cooked. Correct the seasoning, adding pepper and more soy sauce if needed. Serve over steamed white rice.   *—Loraine Berry*

Spicy Honey Mushroom Relish

Makes 1 pint

This sweet and spicy relish is excellent with baked ham.

3 tablespoons butter
1 pound small whole honey mushrooms
1 teaspoon flour
⅛ teaspoon ground nutmeg
¼ teaspoon freshly grated ginger
1 tablespoon brown sugar
½ cup dry sherry
Salt

Melt the butter in a heavy sauté pan or skillet and sauté the mushrooms for 7 minutes. Blend in the flour, spices, and sugar. Stir the sherry in gently and cook slowly for 10 minutes. Add salt to taste and serve immediately.
      —Kitchen Magic with Mushrooms

Matsutake
(Tricholoma magnivelare, formerly Armillaria ponderosa)

Matsutake:
from the depth of the pine forest,
the voice of the hawk.
—Koya

FOR A UNIQUE flavor, try the *matsutake*. This heavy white or brown meaty delight has a thick cottonlike partial veil. The surface is smooth and dry, the stem short and broad. With age, the cap and stem develop rusty stains where bruised. But it is the odor that identifies this mushroom. It is very spicy and clean, like no other foodstuff. Japanese chefs treasure this delicacy, and their preparations reveal how to bring out its strong fragrance and individual flavor.

Matsutake means "pine mushroom." It grows most abundantly along the coast of the state of Washington, where enough is found to permit commercial exportation for sale in Asian markets at high prices. It can also be found in Canada, Oregon, Idaho, and Northern California. It was formerly known as *Armillaria ponderosa*.

In Japan, another mushroom, *Armillaria matsutake,* is collected wild and sold for extravagant prices in marketplaces, where it is beautifully arranged for sale in plastic-covered containers decorated with green leaves. It does not look like *T. magnivelare*. The cap is dark brown, scaled, and bell-shaped, and perches atop a massive round stem that looks like the cut section of a ripe sugar-cane stalk. The few people I've met who have tried it say its taste resembles *T. magnivelare*. Both are prepared the same way.

In Japan and Okinawa, this treasured delicacy is threatened with extinction. The pine forests which are needed for its growth are being decimated by nematodes which attack the roothairs of the trees. Studies are being vigorously conducted to determine how to control this infestation.

When shopping for *matsutakes,* select firm intact mushrooms in prime condition. They should have a decidedly spicy odor. A somewhat rusty discoloration is to be expected.

Cleaning

Remove any soil with water, sparing the underside from soaking. The top and stem are smooth and easily cleaned with a mushroom brush. The bottom of the stem is usually impregnated with soil. Trim and discard.

Cooking

Try marinating *matsutakes* for 10 minutes in soy sauce, dry sherry or sugar, and good-quality bland oil. Then roast them on a grill until golden brown and serve alongside a main course. *Matsutakes* will do wonders for chicken broth and stir-fried dishes. Cut both stem and cap in small pieces, as this mushroom is firm and chewy. It has a magnificent penetrating unique flavor not like anything else: spicy, but not peppery.

When making rice, quickly lift the lid of the cooking pot and throw in a handful of *matsutake* bits. Replace the lid to allow the rice and mushrooms to harmonize inside the pot. This elevates a bland grain to ethereal heights.

Matsutakes blend well with chicken or fish. Even when frozen for a whole year, they retain most of their original zesty flavor.

Fresh or frozen mushrooms may be used interchangeably in all recipes.

Preserving

Slice or dice for freezing. Our Japanese friends wrap whole mushrooms in aluminum foil, then place them carefully in plastic bags prior to freezing.

The flavor of *matsutakes* suffers when subjected to drying, although they may still add interest to culinary dishes.

Pickled Matsutakes

Serves 4 as an appetizer

Pickled *matsutakes* can be used as a relish with almost any food.

1 pound *matsutakes,* cut into ⅜-inch slices
4 green onions, minced
3 tablespoons dry sherry
3 tablespoons fresh lemon juice
2 tablespoons sugar
1 tablespoon *tamari* or soy sauce
½ teaspoon salt

Preheat an oven broiler and broil the mushrooms until brown. Combine all the other ingredients in a small saucepan and boil for 5 minutes. Cool. Place the mushrooms in a glass or ceramic baking dish, pour the liquid over, and store in the refrigerator at least 1 day before serving. —Gathered Mushroom Recipes, *College of the Redwoods*

Gomoku Rice

Serves 4 to 6 as a side dish

In Japanese, *gomoku* means rice prepared with five different foods. *Nori* is a nutritious sea vegetable that is available in natural food stores and Asian markets.

Alternate Mushroom: shiitake

3 tablespoons sake
3 tablespoons soy sauce
2 tablespoons sugar
½ cup water
1 large single chicken breast, skinned, boned, and diced
¼ pound *matsutakes,* thinly sliced
½ cup thinly sliced bamboo shoots
1 large carrot, thinly sliced
¼ cup fresh or thawed frozen peas
1 cup short-grain rice
1 small strip *nori*

Place the sake, soy sauce, sugar, and water in a saucepan. Add the chicken and simmer for 7 to 10 minutes or until the chicken is tender. Add the mushrooms and bamboo shoots, and cook a few more minutes. Gently steam the carrot and peas together for 3 minutes.

To cook the rice, in a saucepan rinse the rice two or three times. Measure the amount of water to add to the rice by placing your middle finger on the bottom of the pan and adding water to the first finger joint. Cover and cook for 5 minutes. Immediately after the rice is cooked (before it starts to steam), add the chicken and its cooking liquid, mushrooms, bamboo shoots, steamed carrots, and peas. Cover the rice and continue to steam for about 10 to 15 minutes. Just before serving, mix the ingredients with a wooden spoon.

Toast the *nori* over an open flame with a fork until it becomes green and crisp. Let cool, then crush it in your hand and sprinkle it over the rice and serve. —*Kyoko Yoshida*

Matsutake Cabbage

Serves 4 to 5 as a side dish

A dish of simple ingredients but elegant and complex flavors. Preparation requires low heat and a long cooking time.

Alternate Mushroom: shiitake

4 tablespoons butter
Two 3-inch-diameter *matsutakes*,
    cut into julienne strips
2 tablespoons water
1 head cabbage, cored and cut
    into 8 wedges

Melt 1 tablespoon of the butter in a sauté pan or skillet and add the *matsutake* strips. Be sure to coat the strips with butter. If not well coated, add more butter. Cover and cook over low heat, stirring occasionally, until golden brown. This should take about 20 to 30 minutes.

While this is cooking, melt 3 tablespoons of the butter with the water in another sauté pan or skillet and add the cabbage. Cover and simmer over low heat for about 15 minutes.

Serve the cabbage topped with the *matsutake* strips.

—*Karel Edith and John Lennie*

Ling Cod with Matsutakes

Serves 4 as a main course

Steamed fish, vegetables, and the spicy *matsutake* mushroom combine to make a healthy, low-calorie dish. Serve over white or brown rice.

Alternate Mushroom:
shiitake

4 thick fillets of ling cod or other
    white fish, scored with a knife
4 green onions, sliced
One ¼-inch-thick slice fresh
    ginger, peeled and shredded
¼ pound snow peas
½ pound broccoli, cut into
    florets
1 zucchini, thinly sliced
½ pound *matsutakes,* cut into
    matchstick-sized pieces
¼ cup dry sherry
Salt and pepper
Tamari or soy sauce
Lemon wedges

Place the fish in a cooking pot that fits into a steamer. Top with the onions, ginger, vegetables, mushrooms, sherry, and salt and pepper to taste. Steam over boiling water for 20 minutes, or until the fish is flaky and tender. Serve with *tamari* sauce and lemon wedges.   —Gathered Mushroom Recipes,
College of the Redwoods

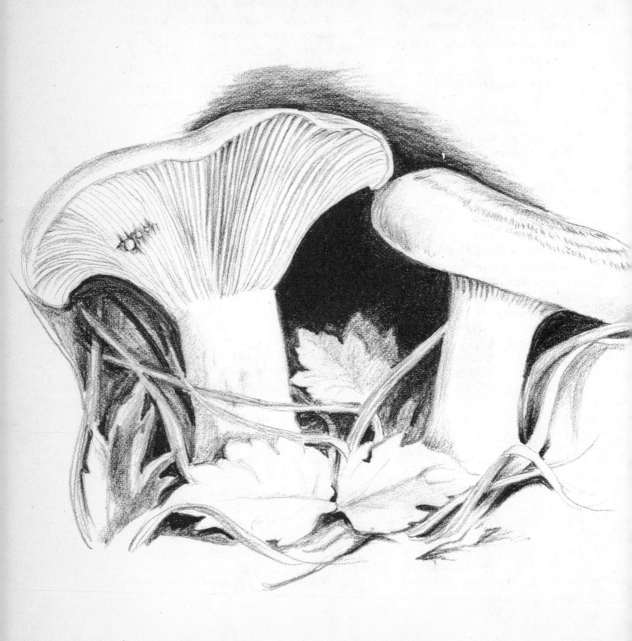

Milky Caps
(Lactarius deliciosus, L. rubrilacteus, L. fragilis)

THE GROUP of mushrooms known as *Lactarius* are commonly called "milky caps." That's because the tissues of these fungi exude a variously colored milk, or latex, when bruised. With time, the color of the latex may change. How lovely it is to discover one of these mushrooms in the forest, and to find that when it is cut, vivid red, white, blue, or orange juice oozes out.

There are many kinds of *Lactarius*. Most are short stemmed, with centrally depressed caps. Three are commonly eaten. *L. deliciosus* ("delicious milky cap") and *L. rubrilacteus* ("bleeding milky cap") can be used interchangeably or together in recipes. These two mushrooms are stout and robust, similar in appearance, and occasionally mistaken for one another. Their flesh is somewhat granular and chalky in consistency. *L. deliciosus* has a cap decorated with concentrically arranged bands colored in differing shades of orange and green. It releases orange-colored latex. *L. rubrilacteus* is zoned with red-brown and orange pigments, and produces red latex.

L. fragilis, the "candy cap," represents a group of closely related species. They are small red-brown mushrooms with watery latex and a fragrant odor identified variously as maple syrup or curry. This becomes more intense when dried. They are found in many habitats, usually late in the mushroom season.

In the eastern United States a stunning blue form, *L. indigo,* is found. It has a pleasant and unusual flavor.

Cleaning

Brush or wipe clean. These mushrooms can be wormy, especially the stems, so check the interiors carefully.

Cooking

Milky caps require a long period of slow cooking. They are best used in conjunction with other foods, as in casseroles. Try making a *Lactarius* loaf with bread crumbs, eggs, herbs, onions, and cheese. Old-timers toss fresh or dried candy caps into soups and stews for flavor or incorporate them into a sweet sauce or pudding to use as a dessert.

Preserving

Sauté *L. deliciosus* and *L. rubrilacteus* in butter and store in the freezer. They can be put up in a favorite pickling mixture and kept in the refrigerator for 1 week. Be sure to parboil them first.

L. fragilis is best dried whole or powdered. It has a smoother texture than the other edible *Lactarius* mushrooms and maintains its flavor for years.

 ## Caramel Candy Cap Custard

Serves 6 as a dessert

Powdered candy caps add a unique flavor to this smooth dessert.

¼ cup dried candy cap
   mushrooms
7 eggs, separated
½ cup honey
4 dashes cayenne
1½ cups milk
¼ cup sugar

Break the mushrooms into small pieces and grind to a fine powder in a blender or food processor.

In a large bowl, beat the egg yolks for 1 minute. Add ¼ cup of the honey, cayenne, powdered mushrooms, and milk. Beat again for 1 minute.

In a cast-iron skillet, caramelize the remaining ¼ cup honey with the sugar until it tests hard in cold water. Quickly pour it into the bottom of a 6-cup ring mold.

In a large bowl, beat the egg whites until stiff, then blend in the yolk mixture and pour into the mold.

Bake in a preheated 300° oven for 30 minutes. Cool on a wire rack and refrigerate for at least 5 hours before unmolding. To unmold the custard, loosen the edges of the custard with a knife. Place in hot water up to the rim of the mold for a few seconds, and quickly turn upside down on a serving plate. Slice and serve.

—John Schaaf

Pickled Milky Caps

Makes 1 pint

In some European countries, milky caps are considered to be the most desirable mushrooms for pickling in vinegar. These piquant treats will keep well for 2 to 3 weeks in the refrigerator.

Alternate Mushrooms:
common store mushrooms, hedgehog mushroom

One ¼-inch-thick slice fresh
    ginger
½ teaspoon caraway seeds
4 allspice berries
½ teaspoon mustard seeds
4 whole peppercorns
4 small dried hot red chilies
1 garlic clove, crushed
6 whole cloves
1 cup water
⅔ cup distilled white vinegar
2 tablespoons olive oil
1 teaspoon salt
1 pound milky cap mushrooms,
    sliced

In a cheesecloth bag, place the ginger, caraway seeds, allspice, mustard seeds, peppercorns, chilies, garlic, and cloves. Tie securely.

In a large pot, simmer the water, vinegar, olive oil, salt, and the cheesecloth bag for 5 minutes. Add the mushrooms and cook for 10 to 15 minutes. Remove the cheesecloth bag. Place the mushrooms in a hot sterilized pint jar and seal.   *—Esther Whited*

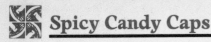

Spicy Candy Caps

Makes about 4 cups

Serve these mushrooms as a relish for meat dishes or as an appetizer. They will keep for several days in the refrigerator.

Alternate Mushroom:
fairy-ring mushroom

1 tablespoon olive oil
1 tablespoon butter
4 cups candy cap mushrooms, stems removed
2 shallots or green onions, minced
1 cup dry sherry
¼ cup chicken broth
Dash of Tabasco sauce
Salt to taste
1 tablespoon minced fresh parsley
½ cup white wine vinegar

Heat the olive oil and butter in a heavy pot. Add the mushrooms and sauté briskly for a few minutes. Reduce the heat and add the shallots, sherry, and chicken broth. Cover and simmer for 15 minutes. Add the Tabasco, salt, parsley, and vinegar. Uncover and simmer for 10 minutes. Cool before serving.

—Kitchen Magic with Mushrooms

Persimmon and Candy Cap Pudding

Serves 6 to 8 as a dessert

A creamy lemon sauce balances the sweetness of this dessert.

1½ ounces dried candy cap mushrooms, stems removed
1 cup water
1 teaspoon fresh lemon juice
1 tablespoon butter
1 cup sliced peeled ripe persimmons
¼ cup milk or more
1 teaspoon vanilla extract
¼ teaspoon ground cinnamon
2 eggs
1 cup sugar
1 cup all-purpose unbleached flour
2 teaspoons baking soda
¼ teaspoon salt
1 cup chopped walnuts

In a medium saucepan, simmer the mushrooms in the water, lemon juice, and butter for 10 minutes. Drain and cool. Place the mushrooms in a blender or food processor along with the persimmons, milk, vanilla, cinnamon, and eggs. Blend until smooth.

Mix the sugar, flour, baking soda, and salt together in a bowl. Add the previously blended mixture in small amounts. The mixture should not be thick. If too thick, add more milk. Add the walnuts.

Pour the batter into a buttered 8-by-12-inch baking dish. Bake in a preheated 300° oven for 45 minutes to 1 hour. To test for doneness, insert a knife in the center of the pudding. If it comes out clean, it is done.

When cool, slice in squares and serve with lemon sauce.　　　　—Kitchen Magic with
Mushrooms

Lemon Sauce

Makes about 1½ cups

½ cup (1 stick) unsalted butter
1 tablespoon flour
3 tablespoons boiling water
½ cup sugar
Pinch of salt
1 egg, beaten
2 tablespoons fresh lemon juice
1 teaspoon grated lemon zest
1 cup heavy cream, whipped

Melt the butter in a double boiler. In a small bowl, make a paste of the flour and water and add it to the butter. Stir in the sugar and salt. Let it cool somewhat. Then add the egg, lemon juice, and lemon zest. When cool, fold in the whipped cream and spoon over the pudding squares.

Morels
(Morchella angusticeps, M. conica,
M. deliciosa, M. esculenta)

BESIDES APRIL showers and May flowers, springtime brings the mushroom hunter some of his or her happiest hours. The small, seductive, yet humble morel becomes the lord of the orchards and forests. So esteemed is this fungus with the hollow pitted hat that its admirers will travel hundreds of miles in its pursuit. Part of the morel's mystique is its ability to blend into the background. That dark, perhaps black, triangle of shadow in the distance. Is it a morel or a pine cone? A piece of bark? A stone? Burned wood? Mushroom collectors will race to it to see if a tasty reward awaits the keenest of eye and swiftest of foot. There are many theories as to the best places to look for these mushrooms, but in the end, everyone admits that morels only grow where the hunter finds them.

A morel of the same species may appear in various colors: *Morchella angusticeps* within the same forest area may be reddish, gray, black, ashen, or brown. It may be isolated or clumped, and has been found in such unlikely places as damp cellars in San Francisco at Christmastime. Unfortunately, it's a Christmas present you can't count on!

Morels emerge as the snow recedes. They fruit most abundantly on disturbed, burned, or recently cleared ground. They may be found under elms that have just died, or in one- to two-year-old wood chip mulch. They also enjoy popping up in fruit orchards. A plentiful crop does not mean that they can be found in the same area in subsequent years, for morels get bored easily and enjoy traveling. Caps usually begin to appear in April in the continental United States, although we have harvested them in the first week in July in the Sierra Nevada. Because of its appearance, the morel is sometimes called "the sponge mushroom."

The classification of the *Morchella* genus intrigues the experts. There is much variation in size and color. To us, differentiation between the species is academic. All kinds are cleaned and cooked in the same manner.

Avoid morels whose caps are soft or mushy, or become granular when rubbed: they are too old and wormy. Morels occasionally contain insect larvae that drop out during the drying process. The mushroom-lovers we know have disregarded this aspect of morel enjoyment. After all, they are very small worms.

Fresh morels are occasionally sold in markets. The price is very high. Select them individually, because each one will be costly. So far, no one has been able to cultivate morels commercially. A company in Felton, California, once harvested them in adequate numbers, but went out of business because they couldn't remove sand from the caps. More recently, a graduate of San Francisco State University developed a technique for growing morels that is now being patented. We hope that his process will soon be converted into a commercially profitable product.

Cleaning

Because of the irregular nature of its surface a morel cannot be rubbed or brushed. You may find this worrisome, wondering about what kinds of things lurk in the dark pits ready to jump into your béchamel sauce. Never fear, most morels are very well groomed, and the pits are very shallow. Try not to use water. Even brief soaking removes their flavor, as with other foods such as strawberries. If you must, run water over them rapidly and cook them at once.

Cut lengthwise or cross-section them to clean out the centers.

Cooking

Large specimens may be stuffed through the hollow base, or halved and packed with fillings. Do not discard the stems. Fry or cook morels whole, especially smaller, younger ones.

It is difficult to describe the famous morel flavor. It is nutty, meaty, and unique whether cooked or dried. There is no substitute for butter to bring out its subtle but treasured character. It adjusts extremely well to a light cream sauce with Madeira wine, which can be poured over chicken breasts or thin slices of veal.

Never eat raw morels or raw morel-like mushrooms such as Helvella lacunosa.

Cooking with Dried Morels

The intensity and character of the morel flavor is not lost in drying. We have used them after three years of storage and found them to be just as aromatic, if not more so, as when fresh.

Reconstitute them in hot water for 5 minutes or simmer them in cream until soft, about 15 minutes, not allowing the cream to boil. Always add the rehydrating liquid to the dish for which your morels are intended. A great deal of the flavor remains in the liquid.

When incorporating dried morels in a recipe calling for fresh specimens, use 3 ounces as the equivalent of 1 pound of mushrooms. Once reconstituted, they should be equal in volume.

Preserving

Morels are easily and quickly dried. You may cut them into smaller pieces or leave them whole. Classically, they are strung like beads on thread using a needle, with a button at the bottom. Hang in a warm, dry place. Dehydrators work well too.

Before placing them in a sealed can or bottle, let them dry for a few days in a paper bag hung in a warm place to allow *all* moisture to escape. Otherwise, mold contaminants will jeopardize your treasures.

Another good way to preserve morels is to sauté them in butter and freeze.

Morel Cracker Crumb Fry

Serves 6 to 8 as an appetizer

Collecting morels in May is a Midwestern American tradition for many admirers of this mushroom. Be sure to keep the mushrooms dry and crisp. Cook small amounts at a time so they can be served hot.

Alternate Mushrooms:
oyster mushroom, puffballs

20 to 30 small morels
1 egg, slightly beaten with 2
    tablespoons cold water
½ cup cracker crumbs
Salt and pepper to taste
5 tablespoons butter
2 tablespoons olive oil

Roll the morels in the egg mixture. Put the cracker crumbs, salt, and pepper in a paper bag. Quickly shake the morels a few at a time in the bag. Melt the butter with the oil in a sauté pan or skillet. Sauté the morels until brown and crisp.   —*Louise Freedman*

Morels Stuffed with Sausage

Serves 10 as an appetizer

Stuffed morels are great finger food for parties. They harmonize with sherry or a red wine such as zinfandel or cabernet sauvignon.

Alternate Mushrooms:
common store mushroom,
shiitake

1 pound finely ground sausage
1 tablespoon minced onion
Salt and pepper to taste
⅛ teaspoon ground nutmeg
1 tablespoon chopped fresh
    parsley
⅓ cup cracker crumbs
20 to 25 large morels, halved
    lengthwise

In a sauté pan or skillet, fry the sausage quickly and break it into small pieces. Add the chopped onion and cook for 2 to 3 minutes. Remove as much fat as possible with a spoon. Add the salt and pepper, nutmeg, parsley, and cracker crumbs.

Fill the morels with the mixture, mounding the filling. Place the mushrooms in a buttered shallow baking dish. Bake for 15 to 20 minutes in a preheated 450° oven.

—Kitchen Magic with Mushrooms

Morels and Buttermilk

Serves 10 as an appetizer

Harry Knighton, founder and executive secretary of the North American Mycological Association, recommends preparing morels this way.

Alternate Mushroom:
puffballs

½ teaspoon salt
⅛ teaspoon ground white pepper
¼ teaspoon paprika
¼ teaspoon sugar
⅛ teaspoon dry mustard
Pinch ground turmeric
¼ teaspoon garlic powder
⅛ teaspoon onion powder
½ cup flour
20 to 25 large morels, halved
   lengthwise
½ cup buttermilk
4 tablespoons butter
2 tablespoons mild vegetable oil

Combine the salt, pepper, paprika, sugar, mustard, turmeric, garlic powder, and onion powder with the flour. Dip the morels in the buttermilk and roll in the flour mixture. Melt the butter with the oil in a sauté pan or skillet and sauté the morels until crisp and brown on all sides. —*Harry Knighton*

Morels Stuffed with Walnuts

Serves 4 to 6 as an appetizer

Morels are great for stuffing—
especially with bacon and
walnuts.

Alternate Mushrooms:
common store mushroom, horse
mushrooom, meadow mushroom

2 shallots or green onions,
    minced
2 tablespoons butter
½ cup bread crumbs
1 bacon slice, cooked crisp and
    finely crumbled
½ cup chopped walnuts
½ cup heavy cream
Salt
10 to 15 large morels, sliced
    lengthwise

In a sauté pan or skillet, sauté the shallots in
the butter until translucent. Stir in the bread
crumbs, bacon, and walnuts. Remove from the
heat and mix in the cream. Add salt to taste.

Stuff the morels, using your fingers. Place
the mushrooms in a shallow buttered baking
dish and bake in a preheated 450° oven for 20
minutes or until they turn brown.

—*Louise Freedman*

Stuffed Morels, Japanese Style

Serves 10 as an appetizer

The stuffing in this recipe is
equally tasty with other
mushrooms. Try filling common
store or *shiitake* mushrooms with
this mixture.

½ pound ground pork
1 small onion, minced
9 canned water chestnuts,
    minced
2 tablespoons soy sauce
⅛ teaspoon five-spice powder
1 tablespoon dry sherry
1 tablespoon arrowroot
20 large morels, halved
    lengthwise

In a mixing bowl, combine the pork, onion,
water chestnuts, soy sauce, five-spice powder,
and dry sherry. Stir in the arrowroot.

Mound as much filling as will fit into the
hollow morels. Arrange the mushrooms in a
large baking pan. Bake in a preheated 450°
oven for 20 to 25 minutes.   —*Louise Freedman*

Morels Stuffed with Panade Paste

Serves 12 to 15 as an appetizer

In this dish, whole morels are filled with a rich bacon-flavored stuffing.

Panade Paste
4 bacon slices, cut into 1-inch slices
1 tablespoon chopped fresh parsley
2 tablespoons butter
½ cup fine bread crumbs
White pepper to taste
⅓ cup half and half or more

30 to 35 morels, large enough to be filled through the stem
3 to 4 tablespoons butter
¼ cup Madeira

To make the panade paste, fry the bacon until very crisp. Remove from the pan with a slotted spoon and drain on a paper towel. Allow the bacon to cool. Blend it in a blender or food processor with the parsley until it is almost a paste.

Melt the 2 tablespoons butter in a small saucepan. Add the bread crumbs, bacon-parsley mixture, and the white pepper. Stir for 1 minute or until the bread crumbs are slightly browned. Turn off the heat and blend the half and half slowly into the bread crumb mixture until it becomes a pliable paste.

Prepare the morels by trimming the stems to accommodate the filling. Fill each morel, using a pastry bag.

Melt 3 to 4 tablespoons butter in a large sauté pan or skillet. Sauté the morels until they are brown on all sides. When nearly done, pour the Madeira over the morels. Quickly turn each morel to coat it with the sauce.

—*Louise Freedman*

Steamed Morels

Serves 4 to 6 as a side dish

Steaming makes morels plump and succulent.

20 to 25 small firm morels
5 tablespoons butter
1 garlic clove, minced
2 teaspoons chopped fresh tarragon
2 tablespoons chopped fresh chives or parsley
Salt and pepper

Steam the morels for 10 minutes. While they are cooking, melt the butter in a saucepan. Add the garlic, tarragon, chives, and salt and pepper to taste.

Place the morels in a serving dish and pour the butter sauce over them.

Save the liquid from the steamed morels for use with other dishes.　　—*Bill Freedman*

Morel Bisque

Serves 4 as a first course

The characteristic flavor of morels is highlighted in this bisque. Add buttery croutons to each soup bowl just before serving, if you like.

Alternate Mushrooms: chanterelle, fairy-ring mushroom, shaggy mane

4 tablespoons butter
1 small onion, minced
1 pound morels, chopped
2 tablespoons flour
3 cups beef broth
2 cups half and half
White pepper to taste
2 tablespoons dry sherry
Salt to taste
2 tablespoons minced fresh
   parsley or chives

In a sauté pan or skillet, melt the butter and sauté the onion and the morels for about 10 minutes. Stir in the flour and cook 2 to 3 minutes. Stir in the beef broth until well blended. Add the half and half and white pepper. Simmer, but do not allow the soup to boil. Just before serving, add the sherry and salt, and sprinkle the parsley on top.

—Louise Freedman

Morels in Madeira Sauce

Serves 4 to 5 as a side dish

Philip Turniey, owner-chef of a restaurant in Mariposa, California, prepared our collected morels in this classic way. He served sourdough bread to dip into the sauce that remained.

1 pound morels, split lengthwise
3 tablespoons butter
¼ cup Madeira
Salt to taste
Chopped fresh chives (optional)

In a sauté pan or skillet, sauté the mushrooms in the butter for 2 to 3 minutes on each side. Remove the morels to a warm serving dish with a slotted spoon. Add the Madeira to the pan. Taste the sauce and add salt. Boil rapidly until the liquid is reduced to the consistency of syrup. Pour the sauce over the morels. Sprinkle the chives on top. *—Philip Turniey, Gardenia*
Cantina Restaurant

Chicken Breasts and Morels

Serves 4 as a main course

Chicken and morels are beautifully matched, especially when served over pasta and accompanied with a dry white wine.

Alternate Mushroom:
chanterelle

2 dozen fresh morels, sliced, or 2 ounces dried morels and ½ cup heavy cream
¼ cup flour
4 single chicken breasts, skinned, boned, and pounded flat
5 tablespoons butter
2 tablespoons oil
2 tablespoons brandy
¼ cup beef broth
¼ cup heavy cream (use the reserved cream if you have used dried morels)
½ teaspoon green peppercorns, crushed
2 tablespoons fresh lemon juice
Salt and pepper

If using dried morels, simmer them in the cream until soft, about 15 minutes. Do not allow to boil. Decant the cream leaving the sediment at the bottom of the pan. Reserve the cream.

Flour the chicken breasts lightly. Heat 2 tablespoons of the butter and the oil in a sauté pan or skillet, and sauté the chicken quickly, about 3 minutes on each side, then remove to a heated pan. Deglaze the pan with brandy. Pour this over the chicken breasts. Place them in a preheated 250° oven while you prepare the sauce.

Melt the remaining 3 tablespoons butter in the same pan. Add the morels and cook until they become semi-dry. Add the beef broth and cream and let it cook down into a sauce. Add the peppercorns, lemon juice, and salt and pepper to taste.

Place the chicken breasts on a warm platter and cover with the sauce just before serving.
—*Louise Freedman*

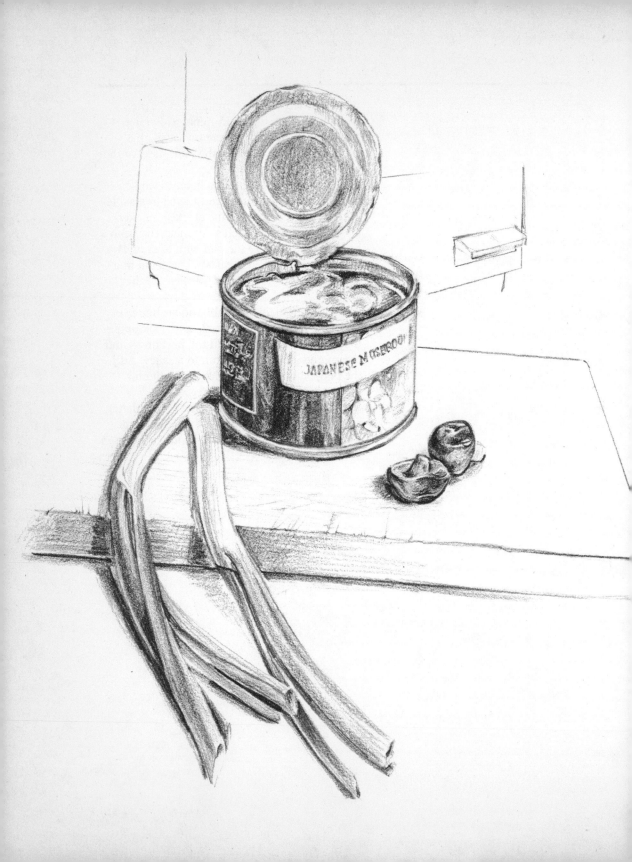

Nameko
(Pholiota nameko)

THE NAMEKO is imported from Japan in small cans for high prices. It is a cultivated mushroom, round in shape, orange in color, gilled, and ½–1 inch in diameter. When you open the can you will find the mushroom suspended in a thick gelatinous soup made of its juice. Purchase only the expensive brands—the cheaper ones are not as good.

Cooking

The *nameko* is usually eaten with steamed rice to which a few drops of soy sauce have been added. Look for them encased in Sushi in Japanese restaurants. When heated, it separates from the material in which it is encased. Add the mushroom with this liquid to *miso* soup.

In Japan it is packaged fresh. We challenge all comers to lift one with chopsticks.

Miso Soup with Nameko Mushrooms

Serves 4 as a first course

Dashi is a broth made from the sea vegetable *kombu,* collected from the icy coastal waters of the islands of Japan. It may be purchased in Asian or natural foods stores as a dehydrated powdered broth. Traditionally, *miso* is made from fermented soy beans with combinations of grains. Red *miso* is usually made with rice. Mixed with *nameko* mushrooms, this soup is delicious.

3 cups water
About 1 tablespoon *dashi*
   powder
3½ tablespoons red *miso*
½ cup diced tofu (optional)
One 7-ounce can *nameko*
   mushrooms

Heat the water in a large saucepan and add 1 tablespoon *dashi* powder, or the amount required to make 4 cups of *dashi* (see the instructions on the *dashi* powder container).

In a small bowl, liquefy the *miso* with 3 to 4 tablespoons of the *dashi* water, then mix with the remainder of the *dashi* water in the saucepan. Bring the mixture to a boil and immediately add the tofu and the *nameko* mushrooms with their liquid. After a half minute or so, when the broth is heated almost to the boiling point, the soup is ready to be served. Do not overcook.

—*Tom Sasaki*

Nameko Mushrooms and Daikon

Serves 4 as a side dish

The peppery, crisp quality of *daikon* contrasts sharply with tofu and *nameko* mushrooms.

Alternate Mushroom: shiitake

¼ cup or more grated *daikon*
One 7-ounce can *nameko* mushrooms, drained, with liquid reserved
2 teaspoons soy sauce or more
One 16-ounce block tofu (optional)
1 sheet *nori,* optional (available in Asian markets)

Mix the *daikon* with the *nameko* mushrooms. Season with the soy sauce; add more according to taste.

If serving with tofu, add a little liquid from the can of mushooms to the *daikon* mixture and mix it with chopsticks. Cut the tofu into ½- to ¾-inch cubes and divide into 4 separate servings, about ½ cup each. Pour the mushroom mixture over each serving.

If using *nori,* toast it over an open flame with a fork until it becomes green and crisp. Let cool, then crush it in your hand and sprinkle it on top of the dish. If the tofu is too bland for your taste, add additional soy sauce.
— *Tom Sasaki*

Oyster Mushroom
(Pleurotus ostreatus)

KNOWLEDGEABLE mushroom lovers all over the world wait until the fall of the year to pursue the robust oyster mushrooms that grow on trees in the wild. Shortly after the first rains of the season, the snow-gray petal-like beginnings of *P. ostreatus* can be found. The autumn forest is brightened with the delicate, young, translucent, eccentrically stemmed caps cascading shelflike from the surface of dead hardwood trees. The cap is scallop shaped and has a delicate aniselike aroma not usually found in oyster mushrooms grown on artifical material. Occasionally, tan caps will be found, and some of these can spread out to 18 inches in diameter, with thick, meaty flesh. It is possible to gather caps from a single log two or three times in one season.

Fresh oyster mushrooms can now be found in supermarkets and farmers' markets alongside our friendly but less-expensive common store mushroom. Cultivated oyster mushrooms are not only sweet tasting but versatile, because they can be used as a subtle flavoring agent in many ways.

A spectrum of colored *Pleurotus* has appeared in the marketplace. Gray, blue, yellow, pink, and white caps will please the eye as well as the palate. Members of our society call it the "designer mushroom." Especially delicious is the dark-capped *P. sajor-caju,* which blends well in a variety of dishes. The stems are tender and tasty, which makes them a good buy.

The most recently introduced cultivated *Pleurotus* is outstanding: it has delicate daffodil-yellow flowerlike caps with pure white stems, and grows in large clumps. One such group could be used as a centerpiece for a dinner table. The almost fruity aroma reminds one of certain zinfandel wines, and this sweet quality is not lost in cooking. Prepared in a baked noodle dish, its pleasant flavor mixes with the other ingredients without losing intensity. Try to buy those which have large caps. The small specimens do not have the same fine flavor. Cook the same way as *P. ostreatus.*

The stems of the yellow *Pleurotus* may be quite bitter to some individuals, in which case they should be removed and discarded.

For do-it-yourselfers, oyster mushrooms can be grown at home on a small scale from kits sold through seed catalogues and gardening magazines.

Occasionally clumps of *Pleurocybella porrigens,* "angels' wings," are found on coniferous wood. These are slender, smaller, short-stemmed relatives of *P. ostreatus.* They are encountered over most the United States. Cook and clean them as you would other *Pleurotus* species.

A few minor intestinal upsets have been reported from eating *Pleurotus* mushrooms. These are usually mild reactions, such as those some of us have had from eating watermelon, cabbage, etc. For this reason, sample a small amount of these mushrooms when you first try them.

Cleaning

Cut off the lower part of the stems of all oyster varieties, especially when using cultivated caps, to remove any shreds of straw or wood. The stems are tough, so discard them. Be certain to rapidly flush out the gill spaces of wild mushrooms. Insects enjoy this sanctuary. Use a minimum amount of water, since *P. ostreatus* is naturally quite moist. Gently press between paper or cloth towels to remove excess liquid. All species of *Pleurotus* are cleaned in the same manner.

Cooking

Oyster mushrooms are used in stir-fried dishes, since the cap is thin and cooks quickly. Asian chefs simply tear the mushroom into desirable sizes before adding it to their woks.

If you prepare a dish that requires a long cooking time, add these mushrooms at the last stage of cooking. Once heated briefly in butter or oil, they add character to a light cream sauce poured over fillets of sole or chicken breasts.

Sometimes very large specimens with flesh more than 1 inch thick are found. These can be cut into large pieces, dipped into slightly beaten eggs, and then rolled in bread crumbs for pan-frying.

Preserving

Store in a freezer after briefly sautéing in butter.

Oyster mushrooms dehydrate rapidly. When used dry, they can be added to a dish without rehydration. Asian stores now offer them in bulk and in packages, fresh or dried.

Oyster Mushroom Chowder

Serves 4 as a first course

A robust soup for a cold night.

Alternate Mushroom:
shaggy parasol mushroom

4 tablespoons butter
½ pound oyster mushrooms,
    coarsely chopped
½ cup minced onions
1 cup cubed peeled potatoes
2 cups milk, scalded
Salt and pepper to taste
Dash of ground mace
Dash of Tabasco sauce
Pinch of dried thyme
2 egg yolks
¼ cup dry sherry
1 cup half and half
Bread cubes browned in butter
    and drained well
Minced fresh parsley

Melt 2 tablespoons of the butter in a large saucepan. Add the mushrooms and onions, and cook for 3 minutes or until tender. Remove with a slotted spoon and keep warm.

Add the remaining 2 tablespoons butter to the pan and slowly cook the potato cubes for 10 minutes or until tender. Gradually stir in the milk. Add the salt, pepper, mace, Tabasco, and thyme. Allow this to come to a boil, then remove the pan from the heat. In a mixing bowl, combine the egg yolks, sherry, and half and half and slowly blend the mixture into the chowder. Add the onions and mushrooms and heat almost, but not quite, to a boil. Taste to correct the flavoring.

Serve at once in soup plates. Float the bread cubes in the soup and sprinkle with parsley.

—Kitchen Magic with Mushrooms

Oyster Mushroom Tempura

Serves 4 as a side dish

Pastry flour makes a lighter batter, but all-purpose flour can be used as a substitute in this recipe.

Alternate Mushroom:
shiitake

1 egg
1 cup very cold water
⅔ cup pastry flour
⅓ cup cornstarch
1 teaspoon baking powder
Salt
1 pound oyster mushrooms, cut
    or torn into large pieces
Oil for deep-frying

Beat the egg slightly in a mixing bowl. Stir in the cold water, flour, cornstarch, baking powder, and salt to make a thin batter. Dip the mushrooms into the batter.

Heat the oil to 375° and deep-fry the mushrooms until golden brown. Drain on paper towels and serve immediately. —*Lois Der*

Chicken Breasts with Oyster Mushrooms in Champagne

Serves 4 as a main course

Alternate Mushrooms:
chanterelle, common store
mushroom, morels

4 single chicken breasts, skinned
and boned
Salt and pepper to taste
3 tablespoons flour
2 tablespoons butter
2 tablespoons light vegetable oil
½ pound oyster mushrooms,
sliced
1 cup heavy cream or half and
half
¼ cup dry champagne
Cilantro sprigs

Pound the chicken breasts between 2 pieces of waxed paper until slightly flattened. Salt and pepper the chicken breasts. Roll them in the flour and shake off excess.

Heat the butter and oil in a large sauté pan or skillet and sauté the chicken over low heat for about 3 minutes for each side. Add the mushrooms and cover the pan for 10 minutes. Add the cream and simmer for 10 minutes, uncovered, over low heat. Transfer the chicken to a serving dish and keep warm.

Add the champagne to the sauce and bring it to a boil, cooking until it becomes creamy. Pour the sauce over the chicken. Garnish with sprigs of cilantro and serve.   *—Linda Scheffer*

Scrambled Eggs with Oyster Mushrooms

Serves 4 as a main course

Most mushrooms may be cooked with scrambled eggs, but oyster mushrooms convert them into an elegant main dish.

1 pound oyster mushrooms,
sliced
½ cup flour
½ cup peanut oil
½ cup slivered shallots or green
onions
8 eggs, beaten slightly
½ teaspoon Tabasco sauce
2 tablespoons chopped fresh
parsley
Salt and pepper to taste
1 teaspoon Asian sesame oil
(available in Asian markets)

Dredge the mushrooms in the flour. Heat the oil in a large sauté pan or skillet. Add the mushrooms and cook until brown. Add the shallots and continue to cook for a few more minutes. Stir in the eggs, Tabasco sauce, parsley, salt, and pepper. Scramble the eggs and sprinkle the sesame oil quickly over the eggs while they are still soft. Serve immediately.   *—Edward Lodigiani*

Stir-fried Oyster Mushrooms

Serves 3 to 4 as a side dish

Oyster mushrooms are incorporated in many Asian dishes. They cook quickly, and are therefore naturals for stir-fries.

Alternate Mushrooms:
common store mushroom, *shiitake*

2 tablespoons peanut oil
½ tablespoon Asian sesame oil
    (available in Asian markets)
One ¼-inch-thick slice fresh
    ginger, peeled and minced
3 garlic cloves, minced
½ pound oyster mushrooms,
    sliced or torn in even pieces
1 cup fresh or thawed frozen
    peas
Pinch of sugar
2 tablespoons chicken broth
2 Chinese-style (firm) tofu cakes,
    cut into cubes
2 tablespoons soy sauce or more

Using a wok or skillet, heat the peanut and sesame oils together until bubbling. Add the ginger, garlic, mushrooms, peas, and sugar and quickly stir-fry for 2 to 3 minutes. Add the broth. Cover and simmer for 3 to 5 minutes. Add the tofu and soy sauce. Cook uncovered for 3 minutes. Serve immediately over rice.

—*Louise Freedman*

Puffballs
(Calvatia, Calbovista, Lycoperdon)

PUFFBALLS COME in many sizes, some as small as a marble and some as large as a basketball. The name "puffball" is used here to refer to three genera of fungi, *Calvatia, Calbovista,* and *Lycoperdon.* Their surfaces may be smooth, covered with small or large warts, or ornamented with spikes. Puffballs are usually white and round, and are attached to the ground with little or no apparent stem.

Puffballs seem to prefer disturbed earth, and enjoy surprising the forager, for they are seldom the prey being sought. The largest ones are members of the genus *Calvatia.* It is estimated that the average mature specimen of *C. gigantea* contains 7 trillion spores stored inside the puffball!

Most puffballs are safe to eat, although rare reactions have been reported. Assuming you have obtained reliable puffballs, you should still follow these steps before eating them:

1. They must be *all white* inside. *Any* shade of yellow or purple makes them inedible or upsetting.

2. When cut, they must have a uniform internal consistency. The external appearance of immature *Amanita* species is similar to puffballs. However, the cap and gills of these unexpanded mushrooms become apparent when the egg-shaped fungi are cut in half. The *Amanita* genus includes the most poisonous species of mushrooms.

Cleaning

Clean them as necessary and dry on paper towels. Some people develop intestinal irritation from the outer covering, so peel this layer with a knife.

Cooking

Some people refer to puffballs as "breakfast mushrooms" because they blend so well with eggs. But they also serve beautifully as side dishes with dinner entrées. A thick slab of puffball develops a lovely golden color when browned in butter. They are often cut into cubes for cooking.

Dip slices in a batter of egg and milk and cover with bread crumbs seasoned with salt and pepper. Sauté in butter and serve with a piquant sauce as the main course for a vegetarian dinner.

Thinly sliced and pan-seared large *Calvatias* can be used as crêpes. Rolled around crab meat, tuna, or other fillings, and held in place with a toothpick, they can be baked for your next party.

Preserving

Chop and sauté them before freezing. The larger species may be sliced and slightly fried, then frozen for later use as crêpes. Separate each portion with waxed paper. Dehydrated puffballs can be powdered for flavoring bland foods.

Parmesan Puffballs

Serves 4 as an appetizer

Hope Miller is the coauthor of the book *Mushrooms in Color.* This is one of her favorite recipes.

Alternate Mushrooms:
boletes, oyster mushroom

1 teaspoon salt
1 cup flour
About 1 pound puffballs, peeled and cut into ½-inch slices
1 egg, slightly beaten with 2 tablespoons water
1 cup freshly grated Parmesan cheese
4 tablespoons butter or more if needed
2 tablespoons oil or more if needed

Mix the salt with the flour. Dip the mushroom slices in the flour, then in the egg, and last, in the cheese. Melt the butter and oil in a sauté pan or skillet and sauté the mushrooms slowly until golden brown. Drain on paper towels. Serve at once.
—*Hope Miller*

Chicken Baked with Puffballs

Serves 4 as a main course

Alternate Mushrooms:
common store mushroom, oyster mushroom

¼ cup flour
1 tablespoon dried tarragon
Salt and pepper to taste
One 2½- to 3-pound chicken,
    cut into serving pieces
¼ cup oil
1 cup dry white wine
2 whole garlic cloves, crushed
3 tablespoons butter or more
About 1 pound puffballs, peeled
    and cut into thick slices

Mix the flour, tarragon, salt, and pepper in a paper bag. Shake the chicken pieces in the bag one at a time.

In a sauté pan or skillet, sauté the chicken in the oil until brown. Remove the chicken pieces from the pan and arrange them in a baking dish. Add the wine to the sauté pan and let it boil for 2 or 3 minutes. Pour the wine over the chicken. Add the garlic cloves to the dish, cover, and bake for 20 minutes in a preheated 350° oven.

While the chicken bakes in the oven, add the butter to the same pan and sauté the puffballs. Toss and gently coat the mushrooms in butter for 7 to 10 minutes or until they turn brown. Add more butter if necessary.

Remove the chicken from the oven and skim off the fat. Add the mushrooms. Cover and continue to bake for 15 to 20 minutes longer.

—Louise Freedman

Puffballs with Scallops and Broccoli

Serves 4 as a main course

Any shellfish or white-fleshed fish may be used in this dish. Serve over hot rice.

Alternate Mushrooms:
common store mushroom, oyster mushroom

One 4-inch puffball
1 cup mild vegetable oil
Pinch of salt
2 cups chicken broth
¼ cup dry white wine
1 pound broccoli
¾ pound scallops
2 tablespoons flour
2 tablespoons butter
2 teaspoons fresh lemon juice
1 cup heavy cream

Peel the puffball and cut it into large pieces. In a sauté pan or skillet, heat the oil to almost smoking (400°). Dip the puffballs a handful at a time for 15 seconds in a large amount of water with a pinch of salt added. Shake the water off of the puffballs and toss them into the hot oil. Fry on all sides until golden brown. Remove with a slotted spoon and drain on paper towels.

In a large saucepan, mix the chicken broth and wine. Reduce the liquid to half the volume by boiling rapidly. Remove and set aside.

Pour out all but 1 teaspoon of the oil from the pan used to fry the puffballs. Chop the broccoli into bite-sized pieces and stir-fry in the pan for 2 minutes. Remove and set aside.

Dust the scallops with the flour. In a sauté pan or skillet, sauté the scallops in the butter and lemon juice until lightly browned. Add the broth and wine mixture and simmer for 3 minutes. Add the cream and simmer to thicken. Add the puffballs and the broccoli. Cook 1 minute more to warm the dish. Season to taste and serve immediately.

—*Shea Moss, from* If You Can't Eat Your Mushroom Take It Dancing

Shaggy Mane Mushroom
(Coprinus comatus)

ADMIRE THE structural delicacy of this stately mushroom, balanced precariously atop its tall, slender white stem. The long white bell-shaped cylindrical cap is covered with large shaggy buff, tan or brown scales, giving it the appearance of a British lawyer's wig. This is why one of its common names is "lawyer's wig." The spores are black. When young, a dainty annular ring is found around the stem; this ring drops down the stem as the mushroom matures. Within twenty-four to forty-eight hours, the borders of the cap begin to liquefy, and the entire cap is converted into a pool of inky black fluid, the origin of the common name "inky cap." Liquefied *Coprinus comatus* was used as writing ink in George Washington's day.

Despite its seemingly frail appearance, this mushroom can generate enough power to perform one of nature's most astonishing weight-lifting acts. Emerging shaggy mane caps may lift asphalt pavement into the air in segments, fragmenting it in the process. They do this by gradually absorbing water and slowly expanding, exerting upward pressure far out of proportion to their fragile substance.

This mushroom contributes its unique robust flavor to some of the tastiest wild-mushroom dishes, such as chicken Tetrazzini and shaggy mane cream soup. For the finest flavor it must be consumed before it begins to liquefy. Eating the dissolving mushroom is not harmful, but the cooked remnants will be slimy and less flavorful than those with solid flesh. Vietnamese villagers invert them in the hollows of empty egg cartons to prevent liquefaction in order to transport them. This allows them to survive for a few days longer. Fortunately, *Coprinus comatus* often fruits in large numbers, affording the collector the opportunity to gather mainly young and unliquefied specimens.

Coprinus micaceus ("mica cap") is a smaller, tawny yellow to reddish-brown member of this genus. In some parts of the country, it is more abundant than the shaggy mane. It is occasionally found growing in clumps from under protective rocks or logs. With a hand lens, shiny, angular, granular crystals may be seen at the apex of the cap. These particles resemble mica, from which the mushroom derives its name. *C. micaceus* can be used as a substitute for *C. comatus,* but it is not as flavorsome.

Some people eat *C. atramentarius,* a close relative of the shaggy mane. This mushroom contains a chemical called coprine, a substance which acts like the medicine Antabuse. As a rule, when alcoholic beverages of any sort are drunk before or after eating these mushrooms, one becomes quite uncomfortable.

Cleaning

Using your fingers or a soft brush and as little water as possible, very gently clean the mushrooms of dirt and debris. Water hastens their deterioration, so they should be cooked immediately. Careful collecting and gentle handling are essential to keep them intact.

Cooking

Do not cut these mushrooms into small pieces. The tissues are tender, and the *Coprinus* cooks quickly. Sauté it in butter with chopped onions, salt and pepper, and add it to soup or pasta. Much liquid is released from the mushrooms when they are heated. Pouring off the fluid for later use will speed up the cooking process.

Its unique aromatic taste is transferred to the other foods and liquid with which it is prepared. Dairy dishes, soups, pasta, and poultry pick up its savoriness exceptionally well.

Preserving

After sautéing for 3 to 5 minutes, place in containers for freezing. Most of their flavor is lost when shaggy manes are dried.

Shaggy Mane Quiche

Serves 6 as a first course

Speed is essential in getting shaggy manes into the pot. One ardent admirer of this mushroom takes a skillet and butter on collecting trips so that the shaggy manes can be eaten where they are found.

Alternate Mushrooms:
chanterelle, common store mushroom, morels

½ recipe pie crust (page 46)
5 to 6 bacon slices, cut into
   1-inch pieces
½ to 1 pound shaggy manes,
   sliced
4 shallots or green onions,
   minced
½ cup freshly grated provolone
   cheese
⅛ teaspoon ground nutmeg
¼ teaspoon salt
Pinch of cayenne
4 eggs, well beaten
2 cups half and half

Prepare the pie crust. Roll the dough out to a 10-inch crust. Line a 9-inch pie pan with the crust. Crimp the edges.

In a sauté pan or skillet, fry the bacon until crisp, then remove it from the pan with a slotted spoon and drain on paper towels. Discard all but 2 tablespoons of the bacon fat and sauté the mushrooms and shallots until the shallots are translucent and most of the mushroom liquid has evaporated.

Spread the bacon over the pie crust. Add the grated cheese, then the mushrooms and shallots. Mix the nutmeg, salt, and cayenne into the beaten eggs. Add the cream. Slowly pour the custard mixture over the bacon, cheese, and mushrooms.

Bake the quiche in a preheated 350° oven for about 35 minutes or until the custard is set and the top is brown.

—Kitchen Magic with Mushrooms

Crêpes Forestière

Serves 8 as a main course

Shea suggests serving this dish
with crisp steamed julienne
strips of carrots, garnished with
watercress.

Alternate Mushrooms:
blewit, common store mushroom

Crêpes
1 cup unbleached all-purpose
  flour
3 eggs, beaten
½ teaspoon salt
2 to 2½ cups milk
Oil

Filling
4 tablespoons butter
1½ pounds shaggy mane
  mushrooms, sliced
1 tablespoon minced fresh basil
Salt and pepper to taste

Sauce

1 medium onion, minced
1 tablespoon butter
1 cup chicken broth
¼ cup dry white wine
1 cup half and half
Salt and pepper to taste

To make the crêpes, place the flour in a mixing
bowl and stir in the eggs. Add the salt and
enough milk to make a batter the consistency
of heavy cream. Let the batter stand for 1 hour
or more.

Brush a crêpe pan or skillet lightly with oil,
then heat the pan until a few drops of water
dropped into it sizzle and steam. Pour in just
enough batter to coat the bottom of the pan,
then tilt the pan to spread the batter thinly and
evenly. Cook over moderate heat until the
edges of the crêpe begin to curl away from the
pan. Turn the crêpe out onto a tea towel by
rapping the pan sharply. Repeat the process
until you have made 16 crêpes.

To make the filling, melt the butter in a sauté
pan or skillet and cook the mushrooms for 5
minutes. Add the basil, salt, and pepper. Roll a
spoonful or two of the mushroom mixture in
each crêpe and fasten with a toothpick. Keep
crêpes warm in the oven while preparing the
sauce.

To make the sauce, sauté the onion in butter
in a saucepan until translucent. Add the
chicken broth, white wine, and half and half.
Cook the sauce over high heat until it is
reduced by half. Add salt and pepper.

When ready to serve, remove the crêpes
from the oven and place on a serving dish.
Remove the toothicks. Pour the sauce over the
crêpes and serve immediately.

—Shea Moss, from If You Can't Eat
Your Mushroom, Take It Dancing

Shaggy Mane Chicken Tetrazzini

Serves 4 to 6 as a main course

This dish was prepared for a mushroom society dinner by Teeda LoCodo, the illustrator of this book, and we are still talking about how delicious it was.

Alternate Mushrooms:
black saddle mushroom, common store mushroom, morels

1 pound shaggy mane mushrooms, sliced in half
4 tablespoons butter
1 pound cooked chicken or turkey meat
1½ tablespoons flour
2 cups chicken broth
1 cup half and half
⅛ teaspoon ground nutmeg
Salt and pepper to taste
¼ cup dry sherry
½ pound vermicelli
¼ cup freshly grated Parmesan cheese

In a saucepan, sauté the mushrooms in 2 tablespoons of the butter for 5 to 10 minutes, or until brown. Remove with a slotted spoon and mix with the chicken meat. Add the remaining 2 tablespoons butter to the same pan and add the flour. Cook and stir for 2 or 3 minutes. Using a whisk, blend the chicken broth into the flour, whisking continually. When the sauce is thick, add the half and half, nutmeg, salt, pepper, and sherry. Continue to cook until the sauce is well blended. Remove from the heat.

Cook the vermicelli in a large amount of boiling salted water until *al dente*. Drain.

Mix half of the sauce with the chicken and mushroom mixture, and the other half with the vermicelli.

Alternate layers of vermicelli with the chicken and mushroom mixture in a buttered baking dish. Sprinkle the Parmesan cheese on top and bake in a preheated 350° oven for 20 to 30 minutes or until bubbling and brown.

—*Teeda LoCodo*

Shaggy Parasol Mushroom
(Lepiota rhacodes)

THOSE WHO enjoy inventing common names for wild foods have named this hearty fungus the "shaggy parasol mushroom," but most collectors know it by its species name, *rhacodes,* pronounced "ra-ko-dees." *Lepiota procera,* a similar, more stately, and taller mushroom avidly sought in the eastern United States and Europe, is simply known as the "parasol mushroom." It is highly favored and highly flavored.

Lepiota rhacodes is found in the San Francisco Bay Area primarily under Monterey cypress and eucalyptus trees. It also occurs on the borders of compost heaps. This mushroom appears shortly after the first rains, and it fruits during the summer along the Pacific Coast after heavy fogs. It occurs worldwide. The Russians consider it their most beautiful mushroom.

L. rhacodes is a large mushroom. Its cap may reach 7 inches across. The cream- or buff-colored top surface is decorated with crisp dark scales arranged in concentric rings or in interrupted patterns. Characteristically the color becomes orange to red-brown when the stem is cut or the tissues are bruised.

The ample stem supports a thick, cushiony partial veil. The bottom of the stem is bulblike, occasionally surrounded by a volvalike border. Before the cap expands, the young brown specimens have long sturdy stems and the top is round, giving it a drumsticklike appearance.

Gills and spores are white at maturity. A very similar mushroom, *Chlorophyllum molybdites,* is found widely distributed in the United States, but is not commonly found in the San Francisco Bay Area. It grows in warm moist areas and produces green spores, but only when mature. This is important to know, since *C. molybdites* can cause significant intestinal distress.

Intense stomach discomfort may occur from eating raw *L. rhacodes.* They should only be eaten cooked. There have also been a few reports of minor reactions to cooked *L. rhacodes.* It would be wise to eat only a small amount of these mushrooms the first time you try them.

Cleaning

Remove sand and humus with a soft brush and a minimum amount of water. Do not overwater them and wash the meaty flavor down the drain.

Cooking

The gills of the mature mushrooms are very fragile and tend to fragment when sliced.

When cooked, these mushrooms turn deep brown. They have the appearance of meat when cut into thick broad slabs and fried in butter or grilled. You may include them in casseroles, meat loaves, long-cooking pot roasts, and with almost any rich sauce. Sautéed, they are superb as a side dish with roasts, steaks, and chops.

The flavor of the dried mushrooms can become very intense when they are reconstituted in hot water. Resoak them in fresh water to reduce some of this pungency. Save the strong liquid to fortify a stew, sauce, soup, or even the same dish.

We recommend a heavy red wine as an accompaniment, such as burgundy, cabernet, barbera, or bordeaux.

Preserving

Dry the caps of *L. rhacodes* and set aside for 1 to 2 years. Like a fine wine, they improve and mellow with age, the aroma becoming increasingly rich. It is recommended that high temperatures be avoided in the dehydrating process. The gills are not crowded, so the drying time will be shorter than for most mushrooms (see information on drying mushrooms, page 11).

Shaggy Parasols with Noodles

Serves 6 as a main course

A simple noodle dish is elevated to new heights by the addition of these hearty mushrooms.

Alternate Mushrooms:
blewit, morels, shaggy mane

4 tablespoons butter or more
1½ pounds shaggy parasol
   mushrooms, chopped into
   chunks not less than ⅓ inch
   thick
4 garlic cloves, minced
Pinches of fresh basil, thyme,
   and parsley
1 pound dried wide egg noodles
¼ cup sour cream
Salt and pepper

Melt the butter in a saucepan and add the mushrooms. Add the garlic, basil, thyme, and parsley. Stew the mushrooms in their own juice over low heat for about 15 minutes. Add more butter if needed.

In the meantime, boil the noodles in a large amount of salted water until tender. Drain. Add the sour cream to the mushroom mixture, then add salt and pepper to taste and pour over the noodles. Serve immediately.

—*Mike Roberge*

Beef and Red Wine in a Clay Pot

Serves 6 as a main course

The shaggy parasol is a strongly
flavored mushroom that will
stand up to long cooking.
Soaking dried mushrooms is
unnecessary for this dish, for the
long slow cooking time makes
them succulent. Serve over
buttered noodles, with a salad
and a green vegetable.

Alternate Mushrooms:
black saddle mushroom,
hedgehog mushroom

1 teaspoon salt
¼ cup flour
3 pounds lean chuck roast, cut
    into cubes
3 tablespoons oil
1 garlic clove, minced
7 to 10 boiling onions
1½ pounds fresh or 3 ounces
    dried shaggy parasol
    mushrooms
1 bay leaf
1 teaspoon dried marjoram
12 peppercorns
2 cups dry red wine
Freshly ground black pepper to
    taste

Soak a clay pot in water for 15 minutes.

In a mixing bowl, mix the salt and flour
together. Roll the meat in the flour. Heat the oil
in a sauté pan or skillet and sauté the meat
until it is browned. Transfer the meat to the
clay pot and add the garlic, onions, mushrooms, bay leaf, marjoram, and peppercorns.
Pour the wine over these ingredients.

Place in a cold oven set to 400° and cook
for 2 hours. Remove the bay leaf before
serving. Add the pepper just before serving.

—*Louise Freedman*

Mushroom Potato Kugel

Serves 6 as a side dish

Kugel is a Middle European dish similar to a pudding. The strong flavor of the dried shaggy parasol mushroom makes this dish a good accompaniment for a beef rib roast or a leg of lamb.

Alternate Mushrooms:
boletes, common store mushroom

1 medium onion, minced
3 garlic cloves, minced
1 ounce dried shaggy parasol
   mushrooms, cut in small
   pieces
4 tablespoons butter
6 medium red potatoes, peeled
1 medium apple, peeled and
   cored
2 eggs, slightly beaten
2 tablespoons cognac
½ cup flour
2 teaspoons salt
1½ teaspoons baking powder
⅓ cup sour cream (optional)

In a sauté pan, or skillet, sauté the onions, garlic, and mushrooms in the butter for 3 minutes. Allow to cool.

Grate the potatoes and apple, then place them in a tea towel and twist it to remove as much liquid as possible. Place the mixture in a large bowl. Add the eggs, onion-mushroom mixture, and cognac. In a separate bowl, mix the flour, salt, and baking powder together and add it slowly to the potato mixture. Do not overmix, but blend well. Place the mixture in a buttered 8-by-8-inch baking pan and bake in a preheated 350° oven for 1 hour or until the top is brown and the edges crisp. Cut into squares and serve with 1 tablespoon of sour cream on top of each portion. —*Louise Freedman*

Shiitake
(Lentinus edodes)

THIS MUSHROOM is the second most widely cultivated mushroom in the world. It has been a popular food source in the cuisine of Asia for hundreds of years. In America, we have enjoyed it in Chinese and Japanese restaurants. Following recent improvements in cultivating techniques, it is rapidly becoming a favorite in markets and on dining tables in the United States and Canada. In addition, people can now grow it at home using simple kits prepared by mushroom specialty companies.

The *shiitake* has a medium-sized, umbrella-shaped, tan to brown cap. The edges of the cap roll inwards. The underside and stem are white. You will find many variations when you shop for this mushroom.

It has been estimated that the origin of *shiitake* mushrooms can be traced to the cretaceous period, over one hundred million years ago. It is found growing wild in the mountainous regions of China, Japan, Indonesia, and Taiwan. The scattering of *shiitake* spores has been traced using typhoon wind patterns as the mushrooms were dispersed from one to the other of these countries. It is not found wild in the United States or elsewhere.

In China it is called *dongo* and *shanku*. When served in Chinese restaurants here it is called "the black forest mushroom." The Japanese call the most highly prized and priced specimens *donko*. These have closed caps. *Koshin* types (spring season variety) have open caps and are less expensive.

The Chinese were the first to cultivate this mildly fragrant mushroom more than six hundred years ago. Yield and quality varied from year to year until scientific techniques were developed. Japanese scientists developed a method of inserting pencil-shaped plugs of mycelial spawn grown from specially selected varieties of *Lentinus edodes* into holes bored in oak logs. Carefully watched over in the forest, the prepared logs carried out the work that supported the entire *shiitake* industry. Today the *shiitake* is grown in the United States as well as in Asian countries on a variety of materials containing cellulose, such as sawdust enriched with rice bran. It is sold fresh as well as dried.

In Japan and China the chemicals found in *shiitakes* have been analyzed for medicinal properties. Extracts have been used in treating cancer, and claims have been made that they reduce cholesterol, enhance sexual power, prolong life, kill viruses, and improve circulation. Most people will be skeptical of such panaceas, but at the very least, this is the most enjoyable way of taking medicine we have experienced. Read *Mushrooms As Health Foods* by Kisaku Mori if you want to know more about the subject (see Bibliography).

Shop with care when purchasing dried *shiitakes,* since there are many grades and prices. The caps may be thick and fleshy, or thin; large or small; cracked on top or smooth. The very thick, cracked-topped *donko* types are expensive, but worth the price. They are meaty and can stand up to any food.

In the United States bottled extracts of *shiitake* are sold for medicinal purposes, and it is packaged as a powder.

Cleaning

Because *shiitakes* grow on wood or other coarse cellulose materials, the fresh mushrooms are very clean. Brush the caps lightly. As a rule, the stems are tough, so cut them off using a knife or scissors. The stems can be used to add flavor to stock.

Cooking

Shiitake mushrooms will enhance the flavor of most foods, except, perhaps, baked ham. It is also tasty by itself, cooked several different ways. It accents vegetables, meats, seafood, poultry, and even other mushrooms. The classic way of handling dried caps is to simmer them in water with a little soy sauce to make a *shiitake* bouillon. Added to a light cream sauce, the *shiitake* is ideal for flavoring pasta dishes.

Reconstitute dried mushrooms by soaking in hot or boiling water for 20 minutes. Save the liquid to include with your food or for another dish. Pour off the liquid at the top to separate it from any debris at the bottom of the dish in which it was soaked.

Preserving

When dried, they store well in closed glass containers.

Steamed Stuffed Shiitakes

Serves 12 as an appetizer

Prepare these mushrooms in a container that fits into a steamer. Save the rich juice and pour it over white rice.

Alternate Mushroom:
common store mushroom

24 large dried *shiitakes,* stems removed
½ pound ground lean pork
1 green onion, sliced fine
1 small slice fresh ginger, peeled and minced
2 tablespoons soy sauce
1 tablespoon dry sherry
1 egg white, slightly beaten
1 tablespoon cornstarch
1 tablespoon chopped fresh cilantro

Soak the mushrooms for 15 minutes in hot water to cover. Drain and squeeze dry; reserve the soaking liquid.

Mix the pork, green onion, ginger, soy sauce, sherry, egg white, and cornstarch.

Mound the stuffing into the mushroom caps. Place in a heatproof dish that will fit into your steamer. Steam for 20 to 25 minutes. Toss the cilantro on top.   —*Louise Freedman*

Chicken Breasts with Shiitakes

Serves 4 as a main course

4 single chicken breasts, skinned and boned
2 tablespoons fresh lemon juice
1½ cups water
5 garlic cloves, minced
One ½-inch slice fresh ginger, peeled and minced
¼ cup soy sauce or more
12 dried *shiitakes,* stemmed and rinsed

Rub the chicken breasts with lemon juice. Arrange the chicken in a baking dish and bake for 15 to 20 minutes in a preheated 400° oven or until the breasts are brown and juicy. Turn the chicken occasionally while cooking.

While the chicken breasts are cooking, pour the 1½ cups water into a medium saucepan. Add the garlic, ginger, soy sauce, and the mushrooms. Simmer uncovered for about 15 minutes. Adjust the taste. If too salty, add more water. If not, add soy sauce.

Place 3 caps over each breast on individual plates and spoon the sauce over each breast.
—*Louise Freedman*

Nancy's Mushroom Soup

Serves 4 to 6 as a first course

The flavor of *shiitakes* is outstanding. In this soup, dried *shiitakes* are cooked with common store mushrooms.

5 cups beef broth
⅔ cup barley, rinsed
7 to 10 dried *shiitakes,* stemmed and rinsed
1 medium potato, peeled and cubed
1 onion, sliced
7 to 10 common store mushrooms, sliced
4 tablespoons butter
2 tablespoons flour
¼ cup dry white wine
1½ teaspoons minced fresh thyme, or ½ teaspoon dried thyme
Salt and pepper

Bring the beef broth, barley, dried *shiitakes,* and potatoes to a boil; reduce to a simmer.

In a sauté pan or skillet, sauté the onion and common mushrooms in the butter until the onion is translucent. Mix in the flour and stir for 1 to 2 minutes. Stir in the white wine and add the thyme. Gradually stir this mixture into the soup using a whisk to prevent lumps from forming. Add salt and pepper to taste. Continue to simmer the soup for 20 minutes or until the barley becomes soft.

—*Nancy M. Connolly*

Chicken in Red Wine with Shiitakes

Serves 5 or 6 as a main course

Alternate Mushrooms:
boletes, shaggy parasol mushroom

12 small dried or 7 fresh *shiitakes,* stemmed
One 4- to 5-pound roasting hen, cut into serving pieces
¼ cup flour
5 to 6 bacon slices, cut into 1-inch slices
10 boiling onions
3 garlic cloves, minced
Soy sauce to taste
1 cup dry red wine
Salt and pepper to taste

If using dried mushrooms, rinse them and set aside. Dredge the chicken in the flour. Fry the bacon in a sauté pan or skillet until crisp. Remove to a paper towel with a slotted spoon. Add the chicken pieces to the pan and brown on all sides. Transfer the chicken to a baking dish with a cover. Add the onions, mushrooms, garlic, bacon, soy sauce, red wine, and salt and pepper. Cover and bake in a preheated 350° oven for 1½ hours or until the chicken is very tender.

—*Louise Freedman*

Szechwan Beef with Shiitakes

Serves 4 to 6 as a main course

The black bean sauce in this recipe is a thick, salty paste made from fermented soybeans. It is available in Asian markets, along with the Asian sesame oil. The *shiitake* mushroom blends well with this special sauce. Serve over rice.

Alternate Mushroom:
oyster mushroom

One 1-pound skirt steak, sliced ¼ inch thick across the grain
One 1-inch piece fresh ginger, peeled and chopped or crushed
3 garlic cloves, chopped or crushed
One 3-inch dried hot red pepper, chopped
Fresh-ground black pepper to taste
½ cup dry sherry
½ pound *shiitakes,* stemmed
1 tablespoon black bean sauce
1 tablespoon cornstarch
1 tablespoon honey or sugar (optional)
¼ cup beef broth
¼ cup peanut oil
Dash of Asian sesame oil
1 medium onion, cut into wedges
½ pound asparagus or broccoli florets, cut ¼ inch thick diagonally
1 tablespoon soy sauce

In a bowl, combine the beef, ginger, garlic, red pepper, and black pepper. Add ¼ cup of the sherry. Stir well and allow to marinate for 1 hour. Cut a shallow cross in the top of each *shiitake* and set aside. In a bowl, combine the bean sauce, cornstarch, honey, and beef broth.

Add 2 tablespoons of the peanut oil to a hot wok or skillet. When hot, add the meat and seasonings. Stir-fry over high heat until just past rare. Remove to a bowl. Add the remaining 2 tablespoons peanut oil and the sesame oil. Add the onion, vegetables, and *shiitakes* and stir-fry 1 minute. Add the remaining ¼ cup sherry and the soy sauce. Cover. Raise the heat and stir until slightly thickened.

—*Rick Kerrigan*

Snow Mushroom
(Tremella fuciformis)

AT PRESENT, the flowery *Tremella fuciformis* is sold in the United States only in its dried form. This fungus (also called "silver ear mushroom" and "white jelly fungus") is available in two colors, white and tan. They are identical in use and taste. According to Dr. Henry Mee, an Asian-mushroom expert, the color depends on where the mushrooms were grown. These relatives of the ear mushroom, *Auricularia polytricha,* are packaged much like dried seaweed. The tissues are paper thin, with ruffled borders.

A second, premium form of *T. fuciformis* can also be purchased in Chinese markets. Easily recognized, they are stemless white chrysanthemum-like growths, 2 to 3 inches in diameter, usually packaged in decorated gold boxes tied with red ribbons. They have a spicy odor. Unfortunately this is quickly lost in cooking.

Cooking

Soak both varieties in hot water for 5 to 10 minutes until they expand to three to four times their original size. Once reconstituted, they look like white flowers in bloom. Added to chicken soup, they provide a velvetlike crunchy textural interest. Alas, there is no flavor to these visually attractive culinary delicacies.

Chinese people enjoy them in rock candy syrup, usually served in the middle of a banquet. You will find them canned in such syrup in Chinese stores.

Snow mushrooms have been traditionally used as a tonic, a freckle remover, and a cure for female disorders. Eat them and enjoy a long and unblemished life.

Chinese Chicken Soup with Snow Mushrooms

Serves 4 to 6 as a first course

The small dried red dates add a subtle sweetness to this soup. They are available in Asian markets.

Alternate Mushrooms:
ear mushrooms, *shiitake*

½ ounce snow mushrooms
1 whole frying chicken
1 green onion
3 to 4 Chinese dried red dates
    (*hoong joe*)
Salt to taste
Soy sauce to taste
2 cilantro sprigs

Soak the snow mushrooms for 5 to 10 minutes in hot water. Drain and set aside.

Place the chicken in a large pot and cover with water. Bring to a boil, then simmer for 45 to 60 minutes or until tender. Halfway through, add the green onion and Chinese red dates to the soup.

Remove the chicken. Cool, then discard skin and fat. Strip all the meat from the bones. Set the meat aside. Discard the onion and red dates. Skim all fat from the broth. Flavor the broth with salt and soy sauce.

Return the meat to the soup. Add the snow mushrooms. Boil 1 minute and then simmer 3 to 4 minutes. The mushrooms should stay crunchy. Float the cilantro sprigs on top of the soup.   —*Lois Der*

Snow Mushroom and Fruit Dessert

Serves 4 as a dessert

This is a delightful dessert to serve after a heavy meal. Be sure to mix the snow mushrooms and the blueberries together just before serving, or the juice from the blueberries will discolor the snow mushroom.

½ ounce snow mushrooms
½ cup light corn syrup
½ cup sugar
¾ cup water
1 small lemon, sliced very thin
3 kiwi fruits, peeled and sliced
1 cup blueberries
Vanilla ice cream

Soak the snow mushrooms in hot water to cover for 5 to 10 minutes. Drain and rinse.

Bring the corn syrup, sugar, and water to a boil. Lower heat and add the drained snow mushrooms and lemon slices. Simmer for 5 to 6 minutes. Drain the mushrooms and lemon slices in a colander. Allow them to cool.

Just before serving, mix the snow mushrooms and lemon slices with the kiwis and blueberries. Serve on top of vanilla ice cream.

—Louise Freedman

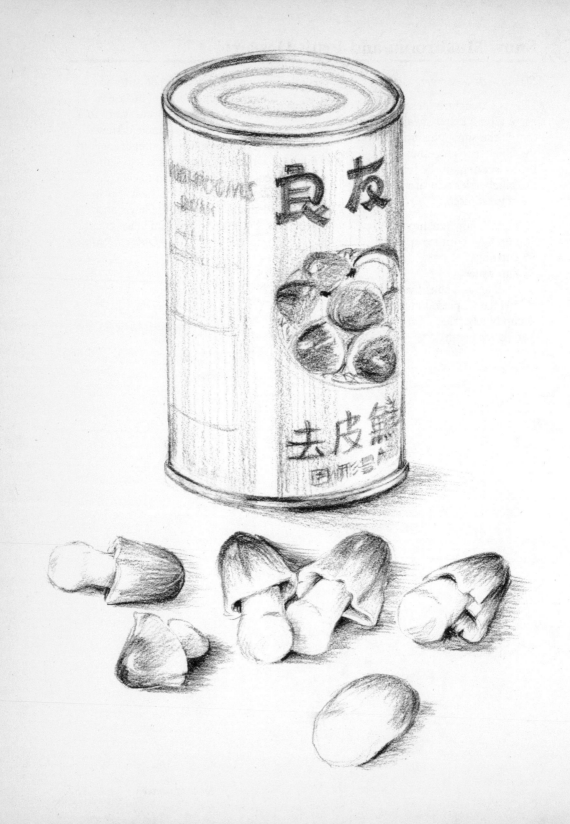

Straw Mushroom
(Volvariella volvacea)

OPEN A CAN of straw mushrooms and out pops Walt Disney's "Danse Chinois" from the movie *Fantasia*. These are mushrooms with happy faces, brown straw hats, and dancing feet.

These jolly mushrooms are called *Volvariella volvacea*. Their common name comes from the rice straw on which they are grown. The straw mushroom, also called "paddy straw mushroom," is cultivated in the hot, steamy climate of Southeast Asia. Attempts to grow them in the southern United States so far have been unsuccessful. They are not widely eaten in the United States, but worldwide they rank third in consumption, just behind *Agaricus bisporus* (the common store mushroom) and *Lentinus edodes (shiitake)*. Indeed, straw mushrooms have been used for food in China for two thousand years.

Baskets of fresh straw mushrooms can be found in the exotic marketplaces of southern China and Asia. They look like tan quail eggs. They are harvested in the "egg stage" before the caps have erupted from their confining universal veils. When sold in this condition they are called "unpeeled." Research has shown that these unopened caps contain a more nutritious balance of amino acids than when opened, suggesting that these mushrooms could supplement proteins lacking in the Asian diet. That is why this mushroom is seldom found "peeled," or in its mature state with the cap open.

In the United States, straw mushrooms are available in canned and dried forms. Canned mushrooms can be purchased in Asian markets. The labels of canned straw mushrooms usually state whether the contents are peeled or unpeeled. The unpeeled mushrooms are stronger in taste. Many companies sell the canned product with significant variations in taste and size. Dried mushrooms can be found in Chinese herbal outlets. These have a more intense flavor than those found in cans.

Cleaning

Drain and rinse the canned mushrooms thoroughly before using. Discard the fluid.

Dried straw mushrooms require close examination. Make sure there are no insects present. The appearance and taste of the dried mushrooms are quite different from those of the canned varieties. Even after a cool-water rinse, their strong flavor persists.

Cooking

Experiment using unpeeled straw mushrooms in different dishes. Fluids held within the cocoon are released upon chewing, producing unusual flavors. Do not burn your mouth by eating them too hot, for the liquor inside retains the cooking heat. A slightly metallic "off taste" is found in some brands. Marinating with soy sauce and/or sherry helps to control this.

The peeled variety is mildly tasteful, and it is a delightful surprise to find one hidden under a snow pea in your favorite stir-fry creation. Add canned or dried mushrooms to your dish near the end of the cooking period. They merely need heating for a few minutes before eating.

Preserving

If you don't use an entire can of mushrooms, store the remaining portion in fresh water; it will keep in the refrigerator for several days.

Fried Bean Curd with
Straw Mushrooms and Snow Peas

Serves 4 as a side dish

Fried tofu has a wrinkled look, is golden brown in color, and can be found in most natural foods stores and Asian markets.

Alternate Mushrooms:
oyster mushroom, *shiitake*

1 teaspoon cornstarch or water chestnut powder
1½ tablespoons soy sauce
1 teaspoon sugar
¼ cup water
2 packages fried tofu
¼ cup peanut oil
½ cup thinly sliced bamboo shoots
4 ounces snow peas, strings removed
Dash of salt
One 15-ounce can straw mushrooms, drained and rinsed

In a small bowl, mix the cornstarch, soy sauce, and sugar with the water and set aside. Cut each piece of tofu into long slices, then cut each slice into bite-sized triangles.

Heat 1 tablespoon of the oil in a wok. Stir-fry the bamboo shoots with a sprinkle of water. Remove to a plate with a slotted spoon. Add 1 tablespoon of the oil and stir-fry the peas with a dash of salt until the color changes. Add the mushrooms and stir-fry a few seconds. Add the remaining 2 tablespoons oil and gently stir-fry the tofu. When the tofu is hot, return all the other ingredients to the wok and stir in the cornstarch mixture. Serve immediately.
—*Helen Studebaker*

Straw Mushrooms in Crab Sauce

Serves 4 as a side dish

Pearl Chen is a member of a mushroom society in Hong Kong. Serve this dish along with a main dish, Western style, or together with several other Asian dishes for guests to share Chinese style.

1 cup chicken broth
1 tablespoon cornstarch
1 teaspoon Asian sesame oil
   (available in Asian markets)
1 tablespoon dry sherry
Dash of white pepper
½ teaspoon sugar
1 tablespoon peanut oil
1 garlic clove, crushed
One 15-ounce can straw
   mushrooms, drained and
   rinsed
¼ pound fresh cooked crab
   meat, flaked lightly
2 egg whites, mixed with
   1 tablespoon water
1 tablespoon minced cooked
   ham

Mix the chicken broth, cornstarch, sesame oil, sherry, white pepper, and sugar in a saucepan.

Place a wok or heavy skillet over high heat. When almost smoking, add the oil. Add the garlic and stir-fry until golden. Discard the garlic. Add the straw mushrooms and the crab meat and cook over medium heat for 2 minutes. Remove the mixture to a serving dish with a slotted spoon.

Quickly add the chicken broth and cornstarch mixture to the wok. Beat the egg whites until mixed but not foamy and stir them into the chicken broth mixture. Pour the broth over the straw mushrooms and sprinkle with chopped ham.
—*Pearl Chen*

Straw Mushrooms with Beef

Serves 4 as a main course

The oyster sauce used in this recipe is a thick concentrate made of oysters and soy sauce. It is commonly used in Chinese cuisine and is found in Asian markets. A bottle will keep without refrigeration almost forever.

Alternate Mushrooms:
common store mushroom,
shiitake

½ pound flank steak
3 tablespoons dry sherry
1 tablespoon soy sauce
1 teaspoon sugar
1 garlic clove, minced

Sauce
2 teaspoons cornstarch
¼ cup water
1 tablespoon oyster sauce
½ teaspoon sugar

2 tablespoons peanut oil
1 bunch broccoli, cut diagonally
    into thin strips
¼ cup thinly sliced onion
1 carrot, cut crosswise into thin
    slices
1 cup snow peas
2 tablespoons water
One 15-ounce can straw
    mushrooms, drained and
    rinsed

Cut the flank steak crosswise into very thin strips. In a mixing bowl, combine the sherry, soy sauce, sugar, and garlic. Add the meat and marinate for 20 minutes.

To prepare the sauce, add the cornstarch to the water and mix well. Add the oyster sauce and sugar and blend. Set aside.

To a large wok or skillet over moderate-high heat, add the oil. When very hot, add the meat and marinade. Cook and stir about 2 minutes, or until no longer pink. Do not overcook the meat. Remove the meat from the skillet and leave some of the juices. Add the broccoli, onion, carrot, and peas and stir to coat with oil and juices. Stir in the 2 tablespoons water to create more steam and cover. Cook a few minutes until the vegetables are semi-cooked. Add the mushrooms, stir, and cover. Cook another 2 to 3 minutes.

Stir the sauce and add to the wok, mixing until the liquid thickens. Return the meat to the wok, mixing all together. Serve over white rice.

—*Lois Der*

Truffles
(Tuber aestivum, T. gibbosum,
T. magnatum, T. melanosporum,
T. texensis)

TRUFFLES HAVE been found in Europe, Asia, North Africa, and North America, but only three species are commercially important. They live in close mycorrhizal association with the roots of specific trees. Their fruiting bodies grow underground.

The term "truffle" as commonly used refers to members of the genera *Tuber* and *Terfezia*. There are many other kinds of subterranean fungi, "false truffles," which outwardly resemble the ones we eat. They are far more common than the ones that are collected for food, and some are poisonous.

Truffles are round, warty, and irregular in shape and vary from the size of a walnut to that of a man's fist. The season for most truffles falls between September and May.

The mention of truffles conjures up images of the expensive French black truffle (*Tuber melanosporum*) from the Périgord region of southwest France, used in making pâté de foie gras, or the renowned odorous white truffle (*Tuber magnatum*) of Alba, in the Piedmont district of Italy.

Since the times of the Greeks and Romans these fungi have been used in Europe as delicacies, as aphrodisiacs, and as medicines. They are among the most expensive of the world's natural foods, often commanding as much as $250 to $450 per pound.

Truffles are harvested in Europe with the aid of female pigs or truffle dogs, which are able to detect the strong smell of mature truffles underneath the surface of the ground. The female pig becomes excited when she sniffs a chemical that is similar to the male swine sex attractant. The use of pigs is risky, though, because of their natural tendency to eat any remotely edible thing. For this reason, dogs have been trained to dig into the ground wherever they find these odors, and they willingly exchange their truffle for a piece of bread and a pat on the head. Not a bad trade for the truffle hunter! Some truffle merchants dig for their prizes themselves when they see truffle flies hovering around the base of a tree. Once discovered, truffles can be collected in subsequent years at the same site.

The flavor of the truffle is directly related to its aroma. The chemicals necessary for the odor to develop are created only after the spores are mature enough for release, so they must be collected at the proper time or they will have little taste. This is the only sure indication that the mushrooms are ready to be harvested. That is why animals have proven to be the best means of assuring that the fungi collected will be flavorful.

Although commercial truffles are more plentiful in Europe than in America, fewer are found there now than in the past. A harvest of 2,200 tons was reported in 1890. Three hundred tons were harvested in 1914, but lately only 25 to 150 tons per year have been found. Truffles appear to have predictable life cycles. To ensure future production, appropriate tree seedlings are inoculated with truffle spores, and when the sapling tree is established, it is transplanted to the proper environment, usually a barren, rock-strewn calcific soil. It takes about seven years before the first truffle begins to grow. A bearing tree will produce for about fifteen to thirty years. For the European market to survive it is necessary to regularly replenish the population of truffle-bearing trees. Inoculated trees have been brought to North America, but it is too early to predict how successful these experiments will be.

Truffles are also found in North Africa, in the Middle East, and in North America. On the desert after rainfall, knowledgeable Middle Eastern people collect the "black kame," *Terfezia bouderi,* and the "brown kame," *Terfezia claveryi.* They prefer the darker ones. In Texas, *Tuber texensis* is collected, and in Oregon, the white *Tuber gibbosum.*

Gaining in popularity and comparing favorably with the Italian truffle, the Oregon truffle is harvested in sufficient quantity to support commercial sales. Although the Oregon truffle industry is in its infancy, it commands as much as $150 per pound for its truffles. James Beard claimed that the mature Oregon white truffle could be substituted for European varieties.

Originally found in California, the Oregon truffle grows in association with Douglas fir trees and is a major food source for many small rodents and other mammals. These underground fungi depend on animals to remove them from below the surface of the earth and to disperse the spores that result in the propagation of truffles. Here is an example of complex ecology, in which the tree, the fungus, and the animal depend on each other.

Collecting truffles requires training and experience. A small hand rake or cultivator is used to gently uncover the soil near the base of suspected host plants. As a rule, in the Northwest, these hosts are various kinds of conifer trees. Small freshly made holes at the bases of trees, which are not part of animal tunnels, are excellent indicators that animals have been digging for fungi.

To enjoy the wonderfulness of the variously described pleasure of dining on truffles, you must eat fresh, slightly cooked specimens shortly after they have been harvested. The strength of the truffle flavor decreases rapidly with time, and much of it is lost before some truffles reach the market. However, lovers of these earthly gems advise us that freshly harvested truffles can be purchased in advance from some local specialty stores. Wholesalers cover them with rice on restaurant serving trays in a refrigerated room as soon as they arrive via overnight air freight. The next day they are delivered to the store where your order was placed. When you spend as much money as will be needed for such culinary experiments, try to assure that you get truly fresh truffles.

The Italian white truffle is considered to be superior in smell and taste to the French black truffle. What does a truffle smell like? "A combination of musk, nuts, and ozone," was one observer's description. *T. aestivum,* a black summer truffle found in Germany, smelled to one observer like "a freshly opened can of creamed corn." This black variety is not considered as choice as the other two European truffles. In Italy one Ping-Pong ball–sized Italian truffle has been said to have perfumed an entire apartment. The powerful pungency of this small tuber was such that some of the inhabitants were forced to flee!

Cleaning

Remove any soil from truffles just before eating. They must be washed with water and brushed. The outside must be immaculate since they will be used unpeeled. Dry with a paper towel.

Cooking

The fungus is scraped or grated onto food and into sauces and soups just before eating. Truffle slicers have been especially designed for this purpose. Experts advise that veal, chicken, fish, soufflés, omelettes, pasta, and rice can be glorified with thinly sliced truffles. Cream and cheese sauces avidly take up their flavor.

Insert thin wedges of truffle under the skin of a chicken and store it overnight in the refrigerator before roasting.

A well-known chef prepares a high-quality pâté de foie gras baked with a stainless steel tube running through the center. As soon as the pâté is cooked, he fills the tube with diced uncooked truffles and then removes the tube.

T. magnatum, the most aromatic of the truffles, is crushed in olive oil in Italy, filtered, and dispensed in 3-ounce medicine bottles with eye droppers. Some suspect that the crushed truffles are then packed in cans for sale in foreign markets. Call local cooking schools or specialty shops to locate this juice. Only a few drops are needed to strengthen the flavor of prepared truffles.

Preserving

The pungent odor of a truffle will penetrate the shells of eggs and flavor kernels of rice when stored with them in a closed glass jar placed in a refrigerator. Once the prize truffle has been consumed, the eggs may be enjoyed in an omelette and the rice in pilaf.

Truffles can be frozen for two weeks in a freezer-proof glass jar. Another recommendation is to store them whole in bland oil.

 ## Truffle Butter

The aroma and flavor of truffles are heat sensitive. Truffle butter is a good way to get the most from your aromatic gem since it is not heated.

Finely grate a fresh truffle and add to softened unsalted butter in proportions to suit your taste. Use enough butter so that the mixture is spreadable and not crumbly. Let stand at room temperature for an hour. Spread on crackers, French bread, or baked potatoes. Truffle butter freezes well.
— *Anne B. Marin*

 ## Truffled Eggs

Henry and Wanda are members of the North American Truffling Society in Oregon, which is devoted to the collection and study of truffles. Members have made generous contributions to this book.

Cut an egg carton in half crosswise. Place 1 or 2 (preferably 2) medium truffles in each carton in the middle of the eggs. Enclose the cartons in a plastic bag and seal. Place in the refrigerator. The eggs will be ready for use after 3 days. (Do not keep the eggs in the refrigerator longer than 1 week, as their odor and flavor may become too strong, and the lack of fresh air may cause them to spoil.) The eggs may be used to prepare scrambled eggs, omelettes, or your favorite deviled egg recipe.
— *Henry J. and Wanda A. Pavelek*

Truffle Pâté

Makes 5 cups

This recipe was developed for the Oregon white truffle, but other truffles can be substituted.

1 to 2 ounces truffles
1 cup beef broth
1½ pounds chicken livers
½ medium onion, chopped
1 apple, peeled, cored, and
  chopped
2 tablespoons shallots or green
  onions, minced
¼ cup fresh lemon juice
¼ cup cold water
2 envelopes (2 tablespoons)
  plain gelatin
1 cup (2 sticks) butter, cut into
  pieces
2 tablespoons Triple Sec
1 teaspoon salt
Dash of dry mustard
Ground pepper to taste

Clean the truffles with a soft brush. Dice large specimens to ¼ inch and split small truffles to release the flavor. In a saucepan, bring the beef broth to a boil, then simmer the truffles for 20 seconds. Pour the broth through a sieve into a bowl and set the truffle pieces and the broth aside.

Oil a 5-cup mold or enough small crocks to hold 5 cups. Combine the livers, onion, apple, reserved broth, and shallots in a medium saucepan and bring to a boil over medium heat. Reduce the heat, cover, and simmer for 5 minutes. Blend the lemon juice, water, and gelatin in a small bowl, stirring well until the gelatin dissolves. Pour into the liver mixture and mix thoroughly. Remove from the heat and add the butter a little at a time, blending well after each addition. Stir in the remaining ingredients. Let cool 15 minutes.

Transfer the mixture to a blender or a food processor and purée until nearly smooth. Let stand 10 minutes. Pour into a mold or crock, layering in about 3 layers of truffle pieces. Cover and chill overnight. Even better, allow 24 to 48 hours to develop the truffle flavor in the pâté.   —*Frank and Karen Evans*

Crab and Truffle Salad

Serves 4 as a first course

Mustard Vinaigrette
½ teaspoon Dijon mustard
2 tablespoons sherry wine
  vinegar
½ teaspoon salt
½ teaspoon ground white pepper
6 to 8 tablespoons mild vegetable
  oil

1 to 2 ounces truffles
¾ pound fresh cooked crab meat
1 pound asparagus, or 2 pounds
  broccoli cut into florets
1 lemon, cut into 4 wedges

To make the dressing, combine the mustard, vinegar, salt, and pepper. Add the oil and mix well. Add more mustard, salt, and pepper to your taste.

Place thin truffle slices between chunks of crab on individual salad plates. Arrange the asparagus or broccoli on each plate. Pour the dressing over and garnish with lemon wedges.
—*John and Pat Rawlinson*

Autumn Truffled Potatoes

Serves 6 as a side dish

An attractive and delicious way to serve baked potatoes.

6 russet potatoes
½ to 1 ounce truffles, grated
2 tablespoons heavy cream or
    half and half
Salt and pepper to taste
2 tablespoons butter, melted

Peel the potatoes. Using a zester, "rib" the outside of each potato; cut the bottom so it stands upright. Wrap in aluminum foil and bake in a preheated 350° oven until tender, about 45 minutes. Unwrap and let stand until cool enough to handle.

Cut a cap from the top of the potatoes. Scoop out the pulp, leaving enough of a wall to support the stuffing. Mix the potato pulp with the grated truffles, cream, salt, and pepper. Place the mixture in a pastry bag and pipe it into the cavity of each potato shell. Replace the cap; brush each potato with butter.

Place on a baking sheet. Bake in a preheated 400° oven for 20 minutes or until heated through and golden brown.

—*Sharon Polster, Edible Art*

Maccheroncini alla Boscaiuola

Serves 5 or 6 as a main course

The name of this luxurious dish of pasta with wild mushrooms and truffles translates as "pasta in the style of the wood-cutter's wife."

¼ pound fresh boletes, sliced, or
    a handful of dried Italian
    porcini
2 tablespoons butter
2 cups heavy cream
1 pound *maccheroncini* pasta (or
    any elbow macaroni)
1 fresh white truffle, sliced
1½ cups freshly grated
    Parmesan cheese
Salt and white pepper

If using dried *porcini,* soak for 20 minutes in warm water to cover, then squeeze dry (reserve the soaking liquid and add to the mushrooms later with the cream).

Heat the butter in a large sauté pan or skillet until melted. Add the mushrooms and cook until golden. Stir in the cream; cook until thick enough to coat the back of a spoon. Cook the pasta in a large amount of boiling salted water until *al dente;* drain and add to the sauce. Add the truffle and cheese; toss over low heat. Add salt and pepper to taste and serve immediately.

—*Michael Hart, Donatello Ristorante*

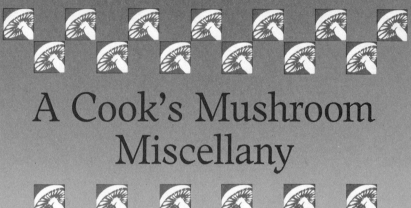

PART FOUR

A Cook's Mushroom Miscellany

What Is a Mushroom?

THE MUSHROOM we see and eat is a part of the reproductive structure of a plant we know as a "fungus." The sole purpose of this organ is to manufacture and spread spores to reproduce its species. The part of the plant we don't usually see, the threadlike *mycelium* living in soil, wood, animal, or plant tissues, constitutes the vegetative portion of the plant. This is the structure of the organism that takes nourishment from living or dead organic material and the earth around it.

Most of the tissues of a fungus are composed of mycelium that forms the parts seen with the naked eye. The mycelium draws its basic food material from the place where it grows. Lacking chlorophyll, which makes the leaves of most plants green, the fungus is unable to manufacture sugar, the backbone for the chemicals needed for life. Carbohydrates such as sugar must be derived from the tissues of other organisms. Acids, iron, calcium, and other inorganic materials are derived from the soil, wood, or animal substances in which the mycelia grow.

Some mushrooms are *parasitic,* such as the oak-tree fungus, *Armillaria mellea* (honey mushroom). Others digest dead tissues from plants and animals. We call these *saprophytes.* A more complicated relationship exists between the root hairs of vascular plants such as trees, which become coated with mantles of mycelia. Such *mycorrhizal* (fungus-root) interminglings improve a tree's vigor and nourish the mushroom as the tree and the fungus exchange nutrients essential for their lives.

What about the food value of mushrooms? Ninety percent of their weight is water. They are low in calories, but high in roughage. Some yellow and orange mushrooms, such as chanterelles, provide Vitamin A in the form of carotene. B vitamins are present, but not Vitamin C. Not much fat or carbohydrate is found. Mushrooms do not form starches. They do contain minerals such as potassium and magnesium, but not much sodium.

In Asia, fungi have been intensely studied in the hope that their use can supplement dietary protein. Experiments have demonstrated that the maximum protein content and the best amino acid balance are found in mushrooms just before the caps expand. We must conclude that the major food value of mushrooms lies in their protein component.

The walls of the mycelium, which make up the solid substance of the mushroom, are composed of *chitin,* the substance forming the exoskeleton of insects. Humans do not have the necessary enzymes to digest this material. Cooking breaks down the mycelial walls releasing the nutritious components of the fungus available for assimilation as food.

Mushrooms As Medicine

In China, mushrooms are valued as much for their healthful properties as for their taste and texture. The Chinese incorporate a wide variety of fungi into their diet for specific medical purposes as well as for general good health. Chinese doctors have been using fungi medicinally for twenty-five hundred years, calling them the "fruit of the earth."

The Chinese do not consider their medicine to be simply folk medicine. Their medical practice is well organized, amply recorded, and long on observation and experience.

In China, the properties of mushrooms have been codified for medical usage. For complete physical and mental health, one ideally balances the *yin* and *yang* elements. The *yin* contains negative qualities and the *yang* positive ones. Using foods to which these elements are traditionally attributed, herbal practitioners construct a dietary program to correct imbalances thought to be causing an illness. Mushrooms are generally in the *yin* group.

Among the fungi used in Chinese medicine are the *shiitake,* ear, snow, oyster, and monkey head mushrooms discussed in this book.

Home Mushroom Cultivation

The hunting of wild mushrooms is so popular that in certain areas in the United States and Europe choice edibles like the chanterelle (*Cantharellus cibarius*) and *Boletus edulis* (*cèpe* or *porcini*) are becoming scarce. It's no surprise that some mushroom fanciers are considering mushroom cultivation as an alternative to long treks in the woods. Cultivation offers several advantages over field collection: it provides mushrooms all year round rather than just during the rainy season; the specimens are low in cost and insect free; poison oak and ticks are avoided; and there is freedom from the suspicion unique to mushroom hunters that a favorite collecting patch has been violated by others.

Growing wild mushrooms would seem to be a simple matter: properly duplicate the conditions under which mushrooms grow in the wild, and success should follow. In practice, however, cultivation using the most carefully controlled techniques can be challenging, and crop failures are not unusual. Still, amateurs employing primitive methods sometimes realize excellent results. An example of a simple cultivation project could involve transplanting a piece of sod containing the fairy-ring mushroom, *Marasmius oreades,* from one lawn to another, or using a piece of wood from a tree harboring oyster mushrooms, *Pleurotus ostreatus,* to innoculate a hardwood log. With time and luck, mushrooms might appear.

But just as likely, competing organisms and improper conditions might interfere with the experiment, yielding poor results. To produce mushrooms, growers use pure cultures and composts, and temperatures and moisture levels are carefully tailored to the needs of each particular mushroom.

At this time, there are about a dozen kinds of mushrooms that can be fairly easily grown. Seven are mentioned here. At the head of the list is the familiar common store mushroom, *Agaricus bisporus,* and its cousin, *A. bitorquis.* Both are usually grown on composted horse manure. Interestingly, the same growth material is also used to cultivate the shaggy mane, or inky cap (*Coprinus comatus*). The easiest of the wild mushrooms to grow is *Pleurotus ostreatus,* the oyster mushroom, which can be brought to fruit in less than three weeks. *Shiitakes* (*Lentinus edodes*) and *enokis* (*Flammulina velutipes*) are similar to the oyster mushroom in that they grow on wood. They can be cultivated on oak and alder logs, but in California they are typically grown on sterilized logs made of hardwood sawdust and rice bran. Finally, the attractive purple mushroom known as the blewit (*Clitocybe nuda*) can be cultivated outdoors in beds of oak leaf mold, although it often takes a year before the mushroom caps emerge.

Alas, the *cèpe* and the chanterelle are not found on this list. They are part of a large group of choice mushrooms that cannot yet be grown commercially. These mushrooms live in association with the roots of specific trees, making it difficult to determine and control their growth requirements. But the future holds much promise for these very desirable delicacies. Because of their potential economic value they are the subject of active study, and it is possible that their cultivation will be successfully worked out, perhaps by growing them in plantations with host trees.

Learning to grow mushrooms starts with reading books on the subject (see Bibliography). Much of the equipment needed for mushroom culture can be found at home. But to develop laboratory skills, it is advisable to take a college microbiology course or to find a mushroom club that offers classes in cultivation.

Mushroom growing is a fascinating hobby. It takes time and patience, but ends by delighting the gourmet with a home-grown culinary reward.

—*Fred Stevens*

Mushroom Manners

Mushroom hunting is a highly rewarding hobby. Not only does it get us out into the countryside and expose us to the beauty of nature, but it can often provide a delicious dish for dinner. It is amazing how fast problems fade into the background when a group of beautiful or unusual mushrooms is discovered in the woods. We are fortunate in the United States to have rich, abundant, and varied forests that promote the growth of many different kinds of mushrooms. In an effort to ensure that our forests continue to exist and that we live to enjoy them, here are a few simple guidelines with respect to mushroom collecting.

Everyone is aware that often there are poisonous mushrooms growing among the edible ones, yet one or more people are poisoned every year, mostly as a result of carelessness. Remember this: the fact that you might have collected and eaten mushrooms from the same spot for the last twenty years does not in any way preclude the appearance of poisonous varieties in that area at any time. Do not eat any mushroom unless you are absolutely positive of its identity.

Here are a few additional suggestions. Respect private property. Don't destroy fences or damage plants. We don't want to foster the appearance of more signs reading "Mushroom Hunters Keep Out!" Be judicious in collecting. Keep your fellow hunters in mind. They too would like some chanterelles for dinner. Disturb the soil as little as possible.

Remember that nothing is gained from knocking over mushrooms that don't interest you. Leave them alone. Who knows, there might be someone behind you who is interested in identifying or photographing them. Lastly, please don't contribute to the increasing amount of litter discarded in our forest and waysides. We have all stumbled onto mushroom "kitchen-middens," places where a collector has discarded undesirable mushrooms or trimmed off diseased pieces that look most unattractive and unnatural in the woods or on the roads. These discards persist for a surprisingly long time and often are repulsive in appearance. If you sort and clean your mushrooms before returning home, please don't do it along trails or roadsides where the discards are readily visible. If possible, bury the debris or toss it into the garbage.

These suggestions are meant to add to the safety and pleasure of mushroom hunting, and to help you enjoy a good meal of wild mushrooms. Keep it up! Enjoy it to the fullest! Just keep your fellow collector in mind and help him to enjoy them as much as you do. Good hunting!

—*Dr. Harry Thiers*

WITH OVER five thousand identified mushrooms to select from in the United States alone, probably no book will ever attempt to catalogue all known varieties with reference to culinary uses.

The majority of mushrooms discussed in the main body of this book are those enjoyed in North America and Europe. We have included commercially available Asian species. The mushrooms listed below are more regional, less often found in the wild, and rarely encountered in the marketplace, if at all. They are usually collected and eaten by well-informed and experienced mushroom fanciers. A neophyte should find a knowledgeable and reliable mycophagist associated with one of the many mushroom clubs listed on pages 217-220 for help in exploring the following group of mushrooms.

Each week collections of fine delicacies not previously offered to the public are appearing in the marketplace. Some of the following species, such as *Stropharia rugosoannulata,* are being cultivated at home by individuals, and we have been informed that mushroom growers are experimenting with other varieties that we hope will soon be introduced to the general public.

Not all mushrooms have common names, and some have different regional common names. We have chosen the most popular names for this list. The scientific names of some varieties are not always agreed upon by experts and these names are often changed, but sometimes enthusiasts continue to use the older names.

SCIENTIFIC NAME	COMMON NAME
Agaricus bernardii	
A. crocodilinus	Crocodile agaricus
A. fuscofibrillosus	Bleeding agaricus
A. haemorrhoidarius	Bleeding agaricus
A. rodmanii or *A. bitorquis*	Spring agaricus
Boletus aereus	
B. appendiculatus	Butter bolete
B. badius	Bay bolete
B. barrowsii	Barrow's bolete
B. bicolor	Two-colored bolete
B. mirabilis	Admirable bolete
B. pinicola	Variant of *B. edulis* (*porcini*)
B. regius	Regal bolete
B. zelleri	Zeller's bolete
Cantharellus lateritius	Smooth chanterelle
Clitocybe fragrans	Fragrant clitocybe

C. odora	Anise-scented clitocybe
Clitopilus prunulus	Sweetbread mushroom
Cortinarius armillatus	Bracelet cortinarius
Entoloma abortivum	Aborted enteloma
Gomphus clavatus	Pig's ear
Grifola frondosa or *Polypilus frondosa*	Hen of the woods
Gyromitra gigas	Snowbank false morel
Hericium americanum (also called *coralloides* and *caput ursi*)	Coral mushroom
H. ramosum	Comb tooth mushroom
Hygrophorus russula	Russulalike waxy cap
Leccinum aurantiacum	Orange-capped scaber stalk
L. insigne	Aspen scaber stalk
L. scabrum	Scaber stalk
Marasmius scorodonius	Garlic marasmius
Pholiota aurivella	Butter mushroom
Phlogiotis helvelloides	Apricot jelly mushroom
Pluteus cervinus	Fawn mushroom
Polyozellus multiplex	Clustered blue chanterelle
Polyporus umbellatus	Umbrella polypore
Ramaria botrytis	Red-tipped coral mushroom
Rozites caperata	Gypsy mushroom or chicken of the woods
Russula aeruginea	Tacky green russula
R. cyanoxantha	Charcoal burner
R. delica	Short-stem russula
R. nigricans	Blackening russula
R. vesca	Bare-toothed russula
R. xerampelina	Shellfish-scented russula
Sparassis crispa or *S. radicata*	Cauliflower mushroom
Strobilomyces floccopus or *S. confusus*	Old man of the woods
Stropharia rugosoannulata	Wine-cap stropharia
Suillis brevipes	Short-stalked slippery cap
S. pictus	Painted suillus

☙ Scientific and Common Names of Mushrooms ☙

NOT ALL mushrooms have common names. Some have more than one. Scientific names are sometimes changed, but mushroom enthusiasts frequently refer to them as they were previously known. We have listed some of these alternate names. The mushrooms in this list include those in the main body of the book as well as those listed under "More Edible Mushrooms."

GENUS	SPECIES	COMMON
Agaricus	*arvensis*	Horse mushroom
	augustus	The prince
	bernardii	
	bisporus or *brunnescens*	Common store mushroom, button mushroom, or commercial mushroom
	bitorquis or *rodmanii*	Spring agaricus
	campestris	Field or meadow mushroom
	crocodilinus	Crocodile agaricus
	fuscofibrillosus	Bleeding agaricus
	haemorrhoidarius	Bleeding agaricus
Amanita	*phalloides*	Death cap
Armillaria	*matsutake*	*Matsutake*
	mellea	Honey or oak mushroom
	ponderosa	American *matsutake* or pine mushroom, recently renamed *Tricholoma magnivelare*
Auricularia	*auricula*	Cloud ear mushroom or Judas' ear
	polytricha	Wood ear mushroom, tree ear, or black fungus
Boletus	*aereus*	
	appendiculatus	Butter bolete
	badius	Bay bolete
	barrowsii	Barrow's bolete
	bicolor	Two-colored bolete
	edulis	*Porcini, cèpe,* or king bolete
	mirabilis	Admirable bolete
	pinicola	Variant of *B. edulis*
	regius	Regal bolete
	zelleri	Zeller's bolete
Bovista	various	Puffball
Calbovista	various	Puffball
Calvatia	*gigantea*	Puffball
Cantharellus	*cibarius*	Golden chanterelle or egg mushroom

GENUS	SPECIES	COMMON
	cinnabarinus	Cinnabar-red chanterelle
	lateritius	Smooth chanterelle
	subalbidus	White chanterelle
	tubaeformis	Trumpet chanterelle
Chlorophyllum	*molybdites* or *morgani*	Green-spored parasol mushroom
Clitocybe	*fragrans*	Fragrant clitocybe
	odora	Anise-scented clitocybe
	nuda	Blewit
Clitopilus	*prunulus*	Sweetbread mushroom
Coprinus	*atramentarius*	Alcohol inky cap
	comatus	Shaggy mane, lawyer's wig, or inky cap
	micaceus	Mica cap
Cortinarius	*armillatus*	Bracelet cortinarius
Craterellus	*cornucopioides*	Horn of plenty, trumpet of death, or black chanterelle
Entoloma	*abortivum*	Aborted entoloma
Flammulina	*velutipes*	*Enoki,* velvet foot, golden needle, or winter mushroom
Gomphus	*clavatus*	Pig's ear
Grifola or *Polypilus*	*frondosa*	Hen of the woods
Gyromitra	*gigas*	Snowbank false morel
Helvella	*lacunosa*	Black saddle mushroom
Hericium	*coralloides, caput ursi,* or *americanum*	Coral hericium
	erinaceus	Bear's head, monkey head, pom-pom
	ramosum	Comb tooth mushroom
Hydnum	*repandum*	Hedgehog mushroom or sweet tooth
	umbilicatum	Belly-button mushroom
Hygrophorus	*russula*	Russulalike waxy cap
Lactarius	*deliciosus*	Delicious milky cap
	fragilis	Candy cap
	indigo	Blue milky cap
	rubrilacteus	Bleeding milky cap
Leccinum	*aurantiacum*	Orange-capped scaber stalk
	insigne	Aspen scaber stalk
	manzanitae	Manzanita scaber stalk
	scaber	Scaber stalk
Lentinus	*edodes*	*Shiitake,* black forest mushroom
Lepiota or *Chlorophyllum*	*molybdites*	Green-spored mushroom
Lepiota	*procera*	Parasol mushroom
	rhacodes	Shaggy parasol mushroom or drumstick mushroom
Lepista or *Clitocybe* *nuda*		Blewit

GENUS	SPECIES	COMMON
Lycoperdon	various	Puffball
Marasmius	oreades	Fairy-ring mushroom
	scorodonius	Garlic marasmius
Morchella	angusticeps	Morel or sponge
	conica	Morel or sponge
	deliciosa	Morel or sponge
	esculenta	Morel or sponge
Phlogiotis	helvelloides	Apricot jelly mushroom
Pholiota	nameko	Nameko
	aurivella	Butter mushroom
Pleurocybella	porrigens	Angels' wings
Pleurotus	ostreatus	Oyster mushroom
	sajor-caju	Oyster mushroom
Pluteus	cervinus	Fawn mushroom
Polypilus or Grifola	frondosa	Hen of the woods
Polyozellus	multiplex	Clustered blue chanterelle
Polyporus	umbellatus	Umbrella polypore
Ramaria	botrytis	Red-tipped coral mushroom
Rozites	caperata	Gypsy mushroom or chicken of the woods
Russula	aeruginea	Tacky green russula
	cyanoxantha	Charcoal burner
	delica	Short-stem russula
	nigricans	Blackening russula
	vesca	Bare-toothed russula
	xerampelina	Shellfish-scented russula
Sparassis	crispa or radicata	Cauliflower mushroom
Strobilomyces	confusus or floccopus	Old man of the woods
Stropharia	rugosoannulata	Wine-cap stropharia
Suillus	brevipes	Short-stalked slippery cap
	granulatus	Dotted-stalk suillus
	pictus	Painted suillus
Terfezia	bouderi	Black kame
	claveryi	Brown kame
Tremella	fuciformis	Snow mushroom, white jelly fungus, or silver ear mushroom
Tricholoma	flavovirens or equestre	Man on horseback
	magnivelare	Pine mushroom or American matsutake
Tuber	aestivum	Summer truffle
	gibbosum	Oregon white truffle
	magnatum	Italian white truffle
	melanosporum	French black truffle
	texensis	Texas white truffle
Volvariella	volvacea	Straw mushroom or paddy straw mushroom

COMMON NAMES vary from region to region and among dialects. There are many common names and infinite variations. We have used Dr. Karl Berger's mycological dictionary as a standard (see Bibliography). Some of the foreign names refer to other closely related species. The mushrooms listed do not occur in every country. The mushrooms in this list are those discussed in the main body of this book.

Black Saddle Mushroom
(Helvella lacunosa)

Czech:	uchác
Dutch:	zwarte kluifjeswam
French:	mitre d évêque
German:	Grubenlorchel
Italian:	spugnola
Polish:	piestrzyca
Russian:	lopastnik
Spanish:	oreja del gato
Swedish:	svart hattmurkla

Blewit
(Clitocybe nuda)

Czech:	cirüvka
Dutch:	paarse schijnridder
French:	tricholome pied-bleu
German:	violetter Rötelritterling
Italian:	agarico violetto, prugnolo
Polish:	gaska
Russian:	ryadovka fiolyetovaya
Spanish:	tricoloma
Swedish:	hostmusseron

Bolete
(Boletus edulis)

Chinese:	meiwei niugan
Czech:	hrib smrkovy
Dutch:	eekhoornt jesbrood
Finnish:	herkkutatti
French:	cèpe
German:	Steinpilz
Italian:	porcino (singular), porcini (plural)
Polish:	borowik
Russian:	byelii greeb
Spanish:	rodellón
Swedish:	stensopp

Chanterelle
(Cantharellus cibarius)

Chinese:	liyoujun
Czech:	liska obecná
Dutch:	hanekam, cantharel
Finnish:	kantarelli
French:	girolle, chanterelle commune, chevrette
German:	echter Pfifferling, Eirschwamm
Italian:	gallinaccio
Polish:	pieprznik
Russian:	lisichka
Spanish:	canterela, cabrito
Swedish:	vanligkantarell

Cloud Ear Mushroom
(Auricularia auricula)

Chinese:	yung nge (*A. auricula*), mo ehr, muk nge (*A. polytricha*)
Czech:	ucho jidásovo
Dutch:	judasoor
French:	oreille de judas
German:	Judasohr
Italian:	orecchio di giuda
Japanese:	kikurage
Polish:	uszak bzowy
Russian:	ioodini ooshi
Spanish:	oreja de judas

Common Store Mushroom
(Agaricus bisporus)

Chinese:	mogu
Czech:	zampion pestovany
Dutch:	gekweekte champignon
Finnish:	upea herkkusieni

French:	champignon, boule de neige
German:	Kulturchampignon
Italian:	prataiolo coltivato
Polish:	pieczarka
Russian:	shampinon
Spanish:	champiñón, hongo campesino
Swedish:	svamp

Fairy-Ring Mushroom
(Marasmius oreades)

Czech:	obecná, spicka
Dutch:	weidekringzwam
French:	marasme, faux mousseron
German:	Nelkenschwindling
Italian:	gambe secche
Polish:	twardzeoszek
Russian:	nyegniyuchnik
Spanish:	ninfa
Swedish:	nejlik-broskskivling

Hedgehog Mushroom
(Hydnum repandum)

Chinese:	chijun
Czech:	houby losákovité
Dutch:	gele stekelzwam
Finnish:	suomenorakas
	(H. umbricatum)
French:	pied de mouton
German:	Semmelstoppelpilz
Italian:	steccherino dorato, gallinaccio spinoso
Polish:	kolczakowate
Russian:	gidnoom, yezhevik zholty
Spanish:	hongos con púas
Swedish:	blek taggsvamp

Honey Mushroom
(Armillaria mellea)

Chinese:	mihuanjun
Czech:	václavka
Dutch:	honingzwam
Finnish:	mesisieni
French:	armillaire, pivoulade
German:	Hallimasch, Honigpilz
Italian:	chidini famigliola buona
Polish:	opienka, miodowa
Russian:	opyenok

Spanish:	armilaria, miel
Swedish:	honungsskivling

Matsutake
(Tricholoma magnivelare)

Chinese:	songxon
French:	tricholome chaussé
Japanese:	matsutake
Polish:	rycezyk matsutake
Russian:	ryadovka
Spanish:	hongo matsutake

Milky Cap
(Lactarius deliciosus)

Chinese:	sung rugu
Czech:	ryzec pravy
Dutch:	oranjegroene melkzwam
Finnish:	leppärousku
French:	lactaire délicieux, catalan
German:	echter Reizker
Italian:	agarico deliziosa
Polish:	rydz, mlecza
Russian:	ryzhik
Spanish:	mízcalo, lactario, rebellón
Swedish:	blodriska

Morel
(Morchella)

Chinese:	yangdujun
Czech:	smrz
Dutch:	morielje
Finnish:	huhtasieni
French:	morille, éponge
German:	Morchel
Italian:	spugnola rotonda
Polish:	smardz
Russian:	smorchok
Spanish:	colmenilla, morilla
Swedish:	toppmurkla

Oyster Mushroom
(Pleurotus ostreatus)

Chinese:	hao gu
Czech:	hlíva
Dutch:	oesterzwam
Finnish:	vinoka
French:	oreillette, couvrosse, pleurote en huître
German:	Austernseitling

Italian:	orecchione gelone, agarico ostreato
Japanese:	shimeji, hiratake
Polish:	boczniak ostrygowaty
Russian:	vyeshyenka obiknovyennaya
Spanish:	pleuroto ostreado
Swedish:	ostronskivling

Puffballs
(Calbovista, Calvatia, Lycoperdon)

Chinese:	chenjun, mabo
Czech:	houba pychavkovitá
Dutch:	stuifzam
French:	vesse-de-loup
German:	Stäubling
Italian:	vescia
Polish:	purchawka
Russian:	dojhdyevik
Spanish:	bejín, pedo de lobo
Swedish:	stor röksvamp

Shaggy Mane
(Coprinus comatus)

Chinese:	maotou quisan
Czech:	hnojník obecny
Dutch:	geschubde inktzwam
Finnish:	suomuinen mustasieni
French:	coprin chevelu, goutte d'encre
German:	Schopftintling
Italian:	coprino chiomato
Polish:	czernidlak
Russian:	navoznik byelii
Spanish:	barbuda
Swedish:	fjälig bläksvamp

Shaggy Parasol Mushroom
(Lepiota rhacodes)

Czech:	bedla vysoká
Dutch:	knolparasolzwam
Finnish:	akan sien
French:	lépiote déguenillée
German:	Safranschirmling
Italian:	mazza di tamburo
Polish:	czubajka
Russian:	greeb-zontik-krasnye
Spanish:	apagador matacandil
Swedish:	rodnande fjällskivling

Shiitake
(Lentinus edodes)

Chinese:	shanku, zhau gu, mo-ehr, dongo
Czech:	sii-take
German:	Shiitakepilz
French:	lentin, cortinaire de Berkeley
Japanese:	shiitake, koshìn, donko, danko
Polish:	lyczak shii-take
Russian:	greeb-shiitakye
Spanish:	hongo shii-take

Snow Mushroom
(Tremella fuciformis)

| Chinese: | sewt yee, bok yhee |
| Japanese: | shirokikurage |

Straw Mushroom
(Volvariella volvacea)

German:	Scheidling
French:	volvaire
Dutch:	beurszwam
Chinese:	tsao gu
Japanese:	fukurotake

Truffles
(Tuber gibbosum, T. magnatum, T. melanosporum, or T. texensis)

Czech:	lanyz
Dutch:	truffel
French:	truffe
German:	Trüffel
Italian:	tartufo
Polish:	trufla
Russian:	tryoofel
Spanish:	trufa
Swedish:	tryffel

Mycological Societies
of the United States and Canada

Arkansas Mycological Society
5115 Main Street
Pine Bluff, Arkansas 71601

Asheville Mushroom Club
Nature Center
Gashes Creek Road
Asheville, North Carolina 28805

Association de Mycologues de
    Montreal
5955 rue Labreche (292)
Ville Laval, Province de Quebec
Canada, HOA 1GO

Boston Mycological Club
100 Memorial Drive, c/o Hrbek
Cambridge, Massachusetts 02142

Central New York Mycological Society
E & F Biology, State University of New
    York
Syracuse, New York 13207

Central Washington Mycological
    Society
P.O. Box 2214
Yakima, Washington 98907

Cercle de Mycologues de Montreal
4101 est rue Sherbrooke, No.125
Montreal, Province de Quebec
Canada H1X 2B2

Cercle de Mycologues de Rimouski
University of Quebec
Rimouski, Province de Quebec
Canada

Cercle Mycologues du Saguenay
438 rue Perreault
Chicoutimi, Province de Quebec
Canada G7S 3W9

Cercle de Mycologues de Sherbrooke
University of Sherbrooke
Sherbrooke, Province de Quebec
Canada

Chibougamau Mycological Club
804 5e rue
Chibougamau, Province de Quebec
Canada G8P 1V4

Colorado Mycological Society
3024 South Winona Court
Denver, Colorado 80236

Connecticut Valley Mycological Society
169 Edwards Road
Cheshire, Connecticut 06410

Eastern Long Island Mycology Club
840 Clearview Avenue
Southold, Long Island, New York ll971

Florence Mushroom Club
Sillcoos Station
Westlake, Oregon 97493

Fungus Federation of Santa Cruz
c/o Santa Cruz City Museum
l305 East Cliff Drive
Santa Cruz, California 95062

Glacier Bay Mycological Society
P.O. Box 65
Gustavus, Alaska 99826

Gulf State Mycological Society
4901 Jim Ramsey Road
Ocean Springs, Mississippi 39564

Humboldt Bay Mycological Society
P.O. Box 4419
Arcata, California 95521

Illinois Mycological Association
P.O. Box 767, c/o Farwell
Libertyville, Illinois 60048

Kitsap Peninsula Mycological Society
P.O. Box 265
Bremerton, Washington 98310

Lincoln County Mycological Society
P.O. Box 282
Depoe Bay, Oregon 97341

Long Island Mycological Club
124-01 20th Avenue, c/o Gallagher
College Point, New York 11356

Los Angeles Mycological Society
Biology, 5151 State University Drive
Los Angeles, California 90032

Mendocino County Mycological
  Society
P.O. Box 87
Philo, California 95466

Michigan Mushroom Hunters'
  Association
15223 Marl Drive
Linden, Michigan 48451

Mid-Hudson Mycological Association
Route #3, P.O. Box 355
Highland, New York 12529

Mid-York Mycological Society
130 Roosevelt Drive
Utica, New York 13052

Minnesota Mycological Society
4128 Seventh Street, Northeast
Minneapolis, Minnesota 55421

Montshire Mycological Club
Jones Hill Road, c/o Scanlon
Enfield, New Hampshire 03748

Mount Mazama Mushroom
  Association
417 Garfield Street
Medford, Oregon 97501

Mycological Association of Washington
9408 Byeforde Road, c/o Lutrell
Kensington, Maryland 20895

Mycological Society of America
c/o Sundberg, Botany Dept.
Southern Illinois University
Carbondale, Illinois 62901

Mycological Society of San Francisco
P.O. Box 11321
San Francisco, California 94101

Mycological Society of Toronto
9 Daleena Drive, Don Mills
North York, Ontario
Canada M3A 2L6

Mycological Society of Vancouver
403 Third Avenue, c/o Tamblin
New Westminster, British Columbia
Canada V3L 2Sl

New Hampshire Mycological Society
84 Cannon Gate Road
Nashua, New Hampshire 03063

New Jersey Mycological Society
1187 Millstone River Road
Somerville, New Jersey 08876

New Mexico Mycological Society
1511 Marble Northwest
Albuquerque, New Mexico 87104

New York Mycological Society
562 West End Avenue, c/o Cox
New York, New York 10024

North American Mycological
 Association
3556 Oakwood
Ann Arbor, Michigan 48104–5213

North American Truffling Society
P.O. Box 296
Corvallis, Oregon 97339

North Idaho Mycological Association
Route 3, P.O. Box 55
Hayden Lake, Idaho 83835

Northwestern Wisconsin Mycology
 Society
311 Ash Street
Frederick, Wisconsin 54837

Nutmeg Mycological Society
P.O. Box 530
Groton, Connecticut 06340

Ohio Mycological Society
1513 Northeast River Road
Lake Milton, Ohio 44429

Olympic Mountain Mycological
 Society
P.O. Box 720
Forks, Washington 98331

Oregon Mycological Society
2781 Southwest Sherwood
Portland, Oregon 97201

Oregon Coast Mycological Society
P.O. Box l590
Florence, Oregon 97438

Pacific Northeast Key Council
124 Panorama Drive
Chehalis, Washington 98532

Parkside Mycological Club
5219 85th Street
Kenosha, Wisconsin 53142

Pikes Peak Mycological Society
P.O. Box 1961
Colorado Springs, Colorado 80901

Prairie States Mushroom Club
310 Central Drive
Pella, Idaho 50219

Puget Sound Mycological Society
University of Washington,
Urban Horticulture, GF–15
Seattle, Washington 98195

Rochester Area Mycological
 Association
P.O. Box 22751
Rochester, New York 14692

Snohomish County Mycological
 Society
P.O. Box 2822, Claremont Station
Everett, Washington 98203

South Sound Mycological Society
111 Archwook Drive, No. 448
Olympic, Washington 98502

Southern Idaho Mycological
 Association
P.O. Box 843
Boise, Idaho 83701

Spokane Mushroom Club
P.O. Box 2791
Spokane, Washington 99220

Tacoma Mushroom Club
P.O. Box 99577
Tacoma, Washington 98499–0577

Texas Mycological Society
7445 Dillon
Houston, Texas 77061

Triangle Area Mushroom Club
P.O. Box 17061
Durham, North Carolina 27705

Tri-Cities Mycological Society
Route 1, P.O. Box 5250
Richland, Washington 99352

Wenatchee Valley Mushroom Society
287 North Iowa
East Wenatchee, Washington 98801

West Michigan Mycological Society
923 East Ludington Avenue
Ludington, Michigan 49431

Willamette Valley Mushroom Society
2610 East Nob Hill, Southeast
Salem, Oregon 97302

Wisconsin Mycological Society
Milwaukee Public Museum, Room 614
  800 West Wells
Milwaukee, Wisconsin 53233

Annulus The skirtlike remnant of the partial veil which shields the lamellae (gills) as they produce the spores and protects the spores until they are ready for release. It surrounds the upper part of the mushroom stem below the cap and sometimes slips down. Not found on every mushroom. Also called "annular ring."

Annular ring See *annulus*.

Antabuse A chemical that prevents the human body from breaking down and excreting the by-products of ethyl alcohol. In combination with alcohol, it causes uncomfortable and dangerous side effects (see *coprine)*.

Bulbous Shaped like a bulb, especially at the base of a stem.

Button The rounded, immature stage of a mushroom with a cap, before the cap has expanded.

Cap The top of the mushroom— usually the spore-bearing part. Also called "pileus."

Chitin The dense substance forming the indigestible outer skeleton of insects, and the material from which the walls of the mycelia are made.

Cocoon The egg-shaped immature form of a mushroom, usually as it erupts from the ground, especially in the *Amanita* genus. It is surrounded by the universal veil.

Coprine A chemical found in the *Coprinus* genus, especially prominent in *C. atramentarius*. Responsible for Antabuse-like reactions if ingested within forty-eight hours of drinking any form of alcohol.

Cultivation The collecting, growing, and inoculation of mycelia, onto special growth materials, and the harvesting of mushrooms using controlled methods.

Cup The remnants of the universal veil surrounding the base of certain mushrooms, such as *Amanita* and *Volvariella*. Also called "volva."

Decant To pour off gently from the top of a liquid so as not to allow sediment or solid material to leave the bottom of the container.

Duxelles A method of preparing minced mushrooms for later use (see page 16).

Eccentric Not in the center.

Egg An early stage of growth (see *cocoon*).

Fairy-ring A formation of certain mushrooms, such as blewits and *Marasmius oreades,* which grow in rings moving outward from a central point of origin.

Fibril A fine hair or fiber.

Filament A long fine hair or fiber.

Field guide A book that carefully describes different mushroom species so they can be tentatively identified.

Fox fire   The release of energy visible in the dark, caused by the presence of phosphorus chemical compounds, especially in *Armillaria mellea* (honey mushroom).

Fruiting body   The part of a fungus that bears the reproductive tissues.

Fungus (pl. *fungi*)   A plantlike living organism lacking chlorophyll and usually producing spores.

Genus (pl. *genera*)   A group of related species demonstrating common characteristics.

Gills   Thin sheetlike curtains that usually bear spores. They are radially arranged under the caps of certain mushrooms. Also called "lammellae."

Gyromitrin   A chemical occuring in certain *Helvella* and *Gyromitra* mushrooms which when broken down in the human body forms monomethylhydrazine, a poison.

Hypogeous   Growing underground.

Latex   The liquid that oozes from certain mushrooms when they are cut or bruised, especially *Lactarius*.

Look-alikes   Mushrooms that closely resemble and may be mistaken for other mushrooms.

Mica   A mineral consisting of shiny, transparent, platelike chemical crystals.

Monomethylhydrazine (MMH)   A chemical used for rocket fuel. It is poisonous if inhaled or ingested. It is released from some *Helvella* and *Gyromitra* mushrooms by drying or boiling in water, and is a break-down product in the human body from a

chemical named gyromitrin which is found in these mushrooms.

Mushroom   A structure bearing the reproductive organs of the plant that produce spores.

Mycelium (pl. *mycelia*)   The mass of fine threadlike structures that make up the vegetative, food-gathering portion of fungi.

Mycology   The study of fungi.

Mycologist   A person who has been professionally trained to study fungi.

Mycophagist   One who has a special appreciation for eating mushrooms.

Mycorrhiza (pl. *mycorrhizae*)   The mutually beneficial growing together of mycelia and the root hairs of trees and other plants.

Nematodes   Round-worms of various sizes, frequently parasitic, infesting plants and animals. Usually passes part of its life cycle in the soil.

Parasite   An organism living on and injuring another organism.

Parboiling   The process of boiling food briefly in water.

Partial veil   A sheet of tissue under a mushroom cap. It stretches from the cap margin to the stem, and protects the sporebearing tissues until the spores are mature.

Photosynthesis   The process by which green plants make carbohydrates such as sugar, using water, carbon dioxide, and sunlight.

Pileus   See *cap*.

Pores   Small openings of tubes where the spores are developed, under the caps of certain mushrooms such as polypores and boletes.

Rhizomorph   A solid rootlike cord of mycelial material.

Saprophyte   An organism deriving its food from dead organic matter.

Spawn   Mycelium produced artificially for the purpose of cultivating mushrooms.

Species   The name given to a single kind of organism. Species can be divided into sub-species.

Spore   The seedlike reproductive unit of a fungus, usually of microscopic size.

Stem   The upright pillarlike part of the mushroom, which supports the cap. Also called the "stalk" or "stipe."

Stipe   See *stem*.

Substrate   The material and/or location on which an organism grows and from which growth materials are extracted.

Taxonomy   The scientific classification of organisms based on their similarities and differences.

Teeth   Narrow, round, spore-producing projections hanging from the bottom of the caps of certain mushrooms such as the hedgehog mushroom.

Tendril   A long, slender, coiled extension of a plant, usually used for its support.

Toxicology   The study of poisons and their effects.

Umbonate   A mushroom cap having a rounded mound in the center.

Universal veil   A sheet of tissue surrounding the entire fruiting body until it is ready to expand and disperse spores, seen especially well in the genus *Amanita*. Portions of the universal veil may remain as wartlike masses on the surface of the cap. The bottom portion may persist as a cup, or volva.

Volva   Cuplike remnants of universal veil at the base of the stem or attached to the lower stem in shaggy rings. Also called "cup."

Zoned   Having concentric bands of color, fibers, or scales, as on the surface of the caps of certain mushrooms such as *Lactarius* species.

Arora, David. *Mushrooms Demystified.* Berkeley, Ca.: Ten Speed Press, 1986. A comprehensive guide to the fleshy fungi of the central California coast.

Berger, Karl. *Mycologisches Worterbuch in 8 Sprachen.* Stuttgart, New York: Gustan Fisher Verlag, 1980. Common European names for mushrooms in eight languages.

Bo, Liu. *Fungi Pharmacopoeia.* Oakland, Ca.: Kinoko Co., 1980. Mushrooms used in Chinese medicine.

Bornholdt, Mariana D. "Three Classical Mushrooms of Oriental Cuisine." In *McIlvainea,* Vol. 4, No. 2, pp. 29-32. Ellsworth, Ma.: North American Mycological Assn., 1980.

Delmas, Jacques. "Truffles in France." *Op. cit.,* pp. 5-7.

Escoffier, A. *The Escoffier Cookbook.* New York: Crown Publishers, 1969. A guide to the fine art of cookery.

The Fanny Farmer Cookbook. New York: Alfred A. Knopf, 1984. Basic information on cooking.

Findlay, W.P.K. *Fungi: Folklore, Fiction and Fact.* Eureka, Ca.: Mad River Press, 1982. Historical background for those interested in mushrooms.

Gray, William D. *The Use of Fungi As Food and in Food Processing.* Cleveland, Oh.: CRC Press, 1970.

Griffiths, D.A. *Fungi of Hong Hong.* Hong Kong: Government Printer, 1976. A guide to poisonous and edible mushrooms found in Hong Kong, with emphasis on medical uses.

Harris, Bob. *Growing Shiitake Commercially.* Madison, Wisc.: Science Tech, 1986. A comprehensive manual on cultivating *shiitakes.*

Harper, Herbert. *Harper's Mushroom Reference Guide and Check List.* Herbert H. Harper, 8975 North Shore Trail, Forest Lake, Mi. 55025: 1985. A comprehensive summary based on field guides of fungi found in the United States.

Lang, M., and Hora, F. B. *Guide to Mushrooms and Toadstools.* New York: E.P. Dutton, 1963. A good resource book for Europe and the East Coast.

Lincoff, Gary. H. *The Audubon Society Field Guide to North American Mushrooms.* New York: Alfred A. Knopf, 1981. Many species listed.

Lincoff, Gary, and Mitchel, D.H., M.D. *Toxic and Hallucinogenic Mushroom Poisoning.* New York: Van Nostrand Reinhold Co., 1977. A handbook for physicians and mushroom hunters.

March, Andrew L., and Kathryn G. *The Mushroom Basket.* Bailey, Colo.: Meridian Hill Publications, 1982. Extensive lists of foreign common names.

Miller, Gloria Bley. *The Thousand Recipe Chinese Cookbook.* New York: Atheneum, 1966. An excellent general Chinese cookbook.

Miller, Orson K., Jr. *Mushrooms of North America.* New York: E.P. Dutton, 1978. A good guide to eastern mushrooms.

Montagné, Prosper. *Larousse Gastronomique.* London: Paul Hamlyn, 1961. An encyclopedic reference for food, wine, and cooking.

Mori, Kisaku. *Mushrooms As Health Foods.* Tokyo: Japan Publications Trading Co., 1974. Recent scientific investigations into the properties of *shiitake* mushrooms.

Mushroom: The Journal of Wild Mushrooming. P.O. Box 3156, University Station, Moscow, Id. 83843. A quarterly magazine dealing with contemporary mycology.

Mushroom Newsletter for the Tropics. Hong Kong: Friendship Printing Co., Ltd., c/o Department of Biology, The Chinese University of Hong Kong, Shotin, N.T. A publication of the International Mushroom Society for the Tropics.

Pilát, Albert. *Mushrooms.* Amsterdam: H.W. Bijl, 1954. A guide to the mushrooms of Czechoslovakia, with excellent illustrations.

The Revolutionary Health Committee of Hunan Province. *A Barefoot Doctor's Manual,* Seattle, Wa.: Madrone Publishers, 1977. A guide to traditional Chinese and modern medicine.

Rinaldi, A., and Tyndalo, V. *The Complete Book of Mushrooms.* New York: Crown Publishing Co., 1972. Beautifully illustrated. Worth having in your library. Describes how mushrooms are used in Europe.

Rocky Mountain Mushroom Cookbook. Denver, Colo.: Cookbook Publishers, 1981. The cookbook of the Colorado Mycological Society.

Rombauer, Irma, and Becker, Marian Rombauer. *Joy of Cooking.* Indianapolis, Ind.: Bobbs-Merrill Co., 1975. Almost everything you ever wanted to know about cooking.

Scates, Kit. *Simplified Picture Key to 55 Genera of Gilled Mushrooms.* Post Falls, Id.: 1977. A useful one-page key for quickly recognizing genera on mushroom forays. A must for beginners.

Sharp, Charles W. *Kitchen Magic with Mushrooms.* San Francisco, Ca.: Mycological Society of San Francisco, 1963. The first cookbook of the Mycological Society of San Francisco. Out of print.

Shimizu, Kay. *Cooking with Exotic Mushrooms.* Tokyo: Shufunomoto Co. Ltd., 1977. This book discusses many Asian mushrooms.

Shiosaki, Pauline. *Oft-told Mushroom Recipes.* Seattle, Wa.: Puget Sound Mycological Society, 1969. Excellent recipes for review.

Stamets, Paul, and Chilton, Scott. *The Mushroom Cultivator.* Olympia, Wa.: Agarikon Press, 1983. A practical guide to growing mushrooms at home.

Theirs, Harry D. *California Mushrooms: A Field Guide to the Boletes.* New York: Hafner Press, 1975. An excellent reference for West Coast boletes.

Trappe, James, M. "Truffles in North America." In *McIlvainea,* Vol. 4, No.2, pp. 3-5, Ellsworth, Ma.: North American Mycological Assn., 1980.

Walter, Tony. *Mushrooms & Man: An Interdisciplinary Approach to Mycology.* Albany, Or.: Linn Brenton Comm. College, 1977. A comprehensive symposium covering many aspects of mycology, presented by the leaders of American mycology.

Wild Mushroom Cookery. Portland, Or.: Oregon Mycological Society. One of the early mushroom cookbooks. Very useful.

Index

in hot and sour soup, 112
with *nameko* mushrooms and
daikon, 153
in oyster mushroom stir-fry,
158
Tomato-mushroom sauce, 22
Tortière, 100
Tremella fuciformis. See Mushroom, snow
Tricholoma equestre. See Mushroom, "man on
horseback"
T. flavovirens. See Mushroom,
"man on horseback"
T. magnivelare. See Matsutake,
American
Trifolati, mushrooms, 25
Truffles (*Tuber; Terfezia*), 194–
201
black. *See* Truffles, French
black
black summer (*T. aestivum*),
196, 213
butter flavored with, 198
cleaning, 197
collecting, 195–97
cooking, 197–98
and crab salad, 200
foreign names of, 216
French black (*T. melanosporum*), 195, 213
Italian white (*T. magnatum*),
195, 197, 213

Oregon white (*T. gibbosum*),
196, 199, 213
with pasta, 201
pâté of, 199
with roast turkey, 73
storing, 198
with stuffed baked potatoes,
201
Texas white (*T. texensis*), 213
to flavor eggs, 198
using, *chart,* 14
white. *See* Truffle, Italian
white; Truffle, Oregon
white; Truffle, Texas
white
"Trumpet of death". *See* Chanterelle, black
(*Craterellus*)
Tuber aestivum. See Truffles,
black summer
T. gibbosum. See Truffles,
Oregon white
T. magnatum. See Truffles,
Italian white
T. melanosporum. See Truffles,
French black
T. texensis. See Truffles, Texas
white
Tuna, *ceviche* of, 98
Turkey
roast
with *porcini,* 73
with truffles, 73

Tetrazzini, with shaggy mane
mushrooms, 171

United States, mycological societies in, 217–220

Veal
breast of, and hedgehog
mushrooms, 123
chops
with chanterelles, 86
scallops, with chanterelles, 85
Vegetables, sautéed with hedgehog mushrooms, 121
Vinaigrette, mustard, 200
Vitamins, in mushrooms, 205
Volvariella volvacea. See Mushroom, straw

Walnuts, in stuffed mushrooms,
31, 146

Yogurt-mushroom soup, 33

Zucchini
with *fettuccine* and mushrooms, 97
and mushroom bread, 71

Recipe Index